ENLIGHTENMENT:

the path through the jungle

First published by O Books, 2008
O Books is an imprint of John Hunt Publishing
Ltd., The Bothy, Deershot Lodge, Park Lane,
Ropley, Hants, SO24 0BE, UK
office1@o-books.net
www.o-books.net

Distribution in:

UK and Europe
Orca Book Services
orders@orcabookservices.co.uk
Tel: 01202 665432 Fax: 01202 666219 Int. code
(44)

USA and Canada
NBN
custserv@nbnbooks.com
Tel: 1 800 462 6420 Fax: 1 800 338 4550

Australia and New Zealand
Brumby Books
sales@brumbybooks.com.au
Tel: 61 3 9761 5535 Fax: 61 3 9761 7095

Far East (offices in Singapore, Thailand, Hong
Kong, Taiwan)
Pansing Distribution Pte Ltd
kemal@pansing.com
Tel: 65 6319 9939 Fax: 65 6462 5761

South Africa
Alternative Books
altbook@peterhyde.co.za
Tel: 021 555 4027 Fax: 021 447 1430

Text copyright Dennis Waite 2008

Design: Stuart Davies

ISBN: 978 1 84694 118 4

A CIP catalogue record for this book is available
from the British Library.

Printed by Chris Fowler International
www.chrisfowler.com

O Books operates a distinctive and ethical publishing philosophy in
all areas of its business, from its global network of authors to
production and worldwide distribution.
This book is produced on FSC certified stock, within ISO14001
standards. The printer plants sufficient trees each year through
the Woodland Trust to absorb the level of emitted carbon in
its production.

ENLIGHTENMENT:

the path through the jungle

Dennis Waite

BOOKS

Winchester, UK
Washington, USA

CONTENTS

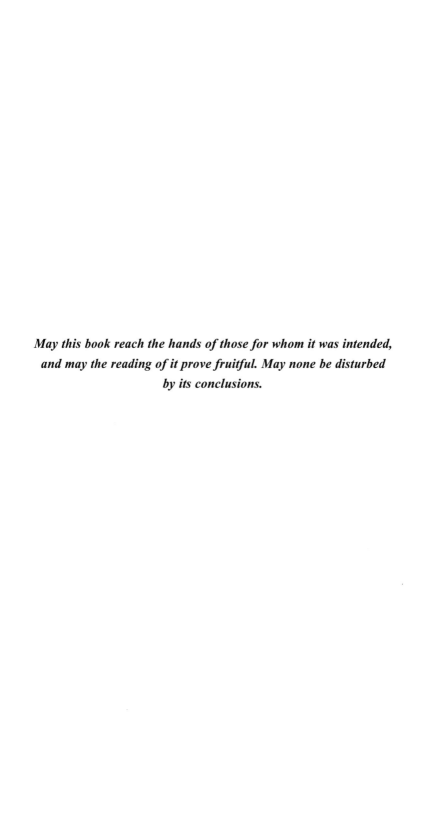

May this book reach the hands of those for whom it was intended, and may the reading of it prove fruitful. May none be disturbed by its conclusions.

I think this is a most valuable work for the serious aspirant who wants to understand the weakness of Neo-Advaita as opposed to the traditional teachings of the great Sages. I agree with the summary of your findings and wish the book well. I am sure it will assist many who are becoming increasingly confused and disillusioned by Neo Advaita, and may turn to the traditional approach.

Alan Jacobs, *President of the Ramana Foundation UK and author of numerous books, including "The Principal Upanishads" and "The Bhagavad Gita".*

When in the Nineties the Neo-Advaita satsang movement burst on the spiritual scene many enlightenment seekers took heart. Here was a teaching in harmony with the fast paced pulse of modern life, one that that did not require effort and promised instant enlightenment. As the new century began to unfold, however, it became apparent to the discriminating that the bloom was off the rose. Although it served to familiarize the public with the idea of non-duality, Neo-Advaita, like so many 'movements', proved to be little more than a lifestyle fad and probably will not rate more than a miniscule footnote in the annals of the spiritual life of the planet.

No harm done? Hardly. As a result of the many ill-considered half-truths it served to propagate it has reinforced any number of enlightenment myths… leaving tens of thousands of seekers disappointed and confused. Dennis Waite's excellent new book, "Enlightenment: the path through the jungle" sets the record straight by comparing Neo-Advaita with traditional Vedanta, a means of enlightenment that has passed the test of time.

This critical but fair book clarifies what enlightenment is and what it isn't according to the traditional definition. It shows why a gradual, systematic, time-tested method of inquiry is necessary. It explains how mixing the relative and the absolute levels causes great confusion. It also provides a valuable service by distinguishing the path of action or Yoga, the techniques used to prepare the mind for enlightenment, from Vedanta, the path of knowledge, the direct cause of enlightenment. It makes it clear that enlightenment is for the mind and that the cursory dismissal of the mind, or the 'story' as it is called in Neo-Advaita, is spiritually counterproductive. It deals with the issues of path and no path, doing and non-doing, appearance and reality, the qualifications necessary for enlightenment, the need for a teacher and other important topics of interest to sincere seekers.

I heartily recommend this book.

James Swartz, *teacher and author of numerous books, including "Meditation: An Inquiry into the Self" and "Self Knowledge", a commentary on Shankara's 'Atmabodha'.*

I welcome Dennis Waite's book *Enlightenment: the path through the jungle* as a breath of fresh air amidst the quagmire of new books on neo-Advaita. Finally, someone has done their homework, and made the effort to create powerful distinctions about what Advaita is and what it isn't. So many are hungry for truth, yet so very few are willing to pay the price. Dennis Waite offers necessary help to sincere seekers who wish to learn how to differentiate between the diamond-like brilliance of authentic Advaita-Vedanta, and the rhinestone approaches represented by popular neo-Advaita.

Mariana Caplan, *Ph.D., author of "Halfway Up the Mountain: the Error of Premature Claims to Enlightenment" (Hohm Press, 1999) and "Do You Need a Guru?: Understanding the Student-Teacher Relationship in an Era of False Prophets" (Thorsons, 2002).*

Over the past ten years or more, many people have been confused by the various interpretations of the teachings of Sri Ramana Maharshi and other recognized gurus in India who teach Advaita according to the traditional values and principles. A number of would-be teachers have misrepresented the teaching, apparently for their own personal glorification. Dennis Waite has presented a clear and informed step by step analysis of what Advaita truly means and shows how the teaching has been subverted by those whose understanding is, to say the least, limited and misguided. He has cleared away the half-truths and the misperceptions about Advaita and shown the correct approach. This is a valuable addition to Advaitic literature and should be read by all those who are perplexed as to the truth of this noble tradition.

The Mountain Path, Tiruvannamalai.

Dennis Waite's newest book is his most succinct and, I daresay, by far his most brilliant and cogent work. This is simply must-reading for any teachers or attendees of the imbalanced pseudo-satsang movement rampant in our era. In a cascading shower of liberating, purifying and healing wisdom, Dennis gives us an elegantly systematic and even beautifully logical presentation of authentic, classically traditional Advaita Vedanta. Clearly, without harangue, yet with ample debunking of many myths, are presented the severe shortcomings of neo-advaita. Some proponents of the latter may find this book 'square.' I found it to be filled with sublime, even sometimes hilarious though subtle wit. A plethora of truly wise, useful distinctions and deliciously quotable quotes are served up here. Any aspirant interested in genuine Self-Awakening is well-served to read *"Enlightenment: the path through the jungle."* Thank you, kindred soul Dennis—with this dazzling bright gem you've helped distinguish True Dharma from falsehood and mediocrity. Namaskaram and love to you and to all beings.

Timothy Conway, *author of "Women of Power & Grace" and the forthcoming 2-volume "India's Sages", and compiler of the multi-faceted internet resource, www.enlightened-spirituality.org.*

Dennis Waite triumphs yet again with the definitive exposition on the fundamental differences in contemporary non-dual teaching, principally between 'traditional' and 'neo' advaita. Elegant and lucid, *"Enlightenment: the path through the jungle"* will dispel all illusions with regard to the myth of quick-fix enlightenment, re-establishing once and for all the respect the traditional teaching truly deserves.

Paula Marvelly, *author of "The Teachers of One" and "Women of Wisdom".*

If you teach, study or practice Advaita, Dennis Waite's latest book on how Advaita should be taught is essential reading. Presenting Advaita in the traditional manner in the West raises difficulties, including the required level of commitment, the inevitable cultural dissonances and the scarcity of accessible, well trained and enlightened teachers. "Enlightenment: the path through the jungle" systematically lays out the relevant issues in sutra format, with a clear indication of the author's views regarding the benefits of the traditional approach and some of the potential faults of the satsang and Neo-Advaitin assumptions and methods. This book will be of interest to the entire Advaita community and is sure to stimulate controversy; with any luck the ensuing dialogue will prove useful and demonstrate the participants' real appreciation of Advaita.

John Lehmann, *Philosophy Foundation, Boston, Massachusetts*

In this instant age, it may be tempting, when you are offered instant enlightenment, to jump on the bandwagon of the latest self-proclaimed 'non-dual sage' and to unquestioningly chant his or her mantra, like some latter day Jehovah's Witness. In the writings of Dennis Waite, we don't find someone professing to be a sage ... we find someone who is offering us the full body of a tradition spanning many hundreds of years, so we can see that this teaching of Advaita is not just a one-dimensional homespun philosophy, but an inspired body of work, built on the foundation of some of the greatest sages who ever lived. To totally ignore this tradition, in favour of a more convenient, though also much more shallow, teaching could be considered an expression of both arrogance and ignorance. In his new work: ENLIGHTENMENT, Dennis Waite rises to the challenge of this modern spiritual dilemma ... confronting the key issues between the traditional and modern approaches to Advaita/Non-Duality head-on. In this regard, he is a lone, rare voice, and should be commended for his diligent work.

Roy Whenary, *author of "The Texture of Being"*

"With Enlightenment: The Path Through the Jungle, Dennis Waite voices a bold and much-needed clarion call. Modern Western Advaita is, in fact, a jungle densely entangled by confusion, complacency and half-measures. If you wish to begin blazing a trail for yourself and for future generations, may I suggest: read this book carefully and then put into action as many of its vital suggestions as you can."

Nathan Spoon, *Advaita teacher and founder of Ganapati-Advaita Ashram and author of "words from an empty boat"*

Foreword

Dennis has written at length about Indian nondualism in **How to Meet Yourself, The Book of One**, and **Back to the Truth: 5000 Years of Advaita**. These books are masterful expositions of Advaita-Vedanta and its more recent offshoots, with Dennis taking you through the teachings as a superbly informed tour guide.

The present book, however, does something altogether different. It is a critique. It critically evaluates the recent form of spirituality known as the Satsang movement from the standpoint of the movement's traditional root teaching, Advaita-Vedanta.

Advaita-Vedanta

The recent and the traditional strands of advaita teaching share a certain body of concepts, but as spiritual activities they see themselves as quite different. Traditionally, Advaita-Vedanta is linked to Hinduism the way Zen is linked to Buddhism. Advaita-Vedanta is the nondual branch of Vedanta, which is the end or goal of traditional Hinduism (there are "dualist" and "qualified-nondualist" branches of Vedanta as well, not covered in this book). As a form of nondual philosophy, Advaita-Vedanta was first systematized by Adi Shankara, and interprets Hinduism's canonical texts, the **Upanishads**, **Bhagavad Gita** and the **Brahma Sutras**, as teaching that reality does not consist of dualism or multiplicity of any kind.

In India, the tradition of Advaita-Vedanta is carried on primarily at the various Hindu monastic organizations called *maTha-s* that follow Shankara's teachings. There are many of these *maTha-s*, and four of them are traditionally said to have been founded by Shankara himself as early as the 5th century BCE. In the West there are no *maTha-s*, but the tradition is easiest to find through the Chinmaya Mission with centers in many Western cities, and the Arsha Vidya Gurukulam, with headquarters in Pennsylvania and a growing number of centers and teachers in the U.S. and Canada.

Advaita-Vedantic teachings proceed by textual exposition and commentary. There is a formal classroom structure, with a preceptor and students. The texts are often taught in graduated order. There are basic texts as well as abstract philosophical texts requiring a great deal of commentary. Verses from the texts are examined, chanted in Sanskrit, translated into English, and commented upon by the preceptor. There is a rich selection of traditional, oral teaching models, chosen in harmony with the level of the text and the class. This method has been in use for thousands of years.

Non-Traditional Advaita

The more recent Western spiritual phenomenon known as the Satsang movement is inspired by well known 20th century Indian teachers such as Ramana Maharshi, Nisargadatta Maharaj, and Hariwansh Lal Poonja, also known as Poonjaji or Papaji. Since the early 1980's scores of Western teachers have appeared in the U.S., U.K., Western Europe and other countries, having met these Indian teachers or having come into contact with their teachings.

Satsang teachers use no texts whatsoever. Instead, they speak from the basis of personal experience. Quite often they report this experience as a result of something that took place when they were with their own teacher, who also did not use texts. Satsang teachers sometimes refer to their teaching as a "gift" or "the truth." In Satsang circles there is the frequent assumption that this gift will be passed on by association or proximity, from teacher to student.

As the Satsang movement gained popularity around the year 2000, observers began to notice differences emerge. Some teachers mainly influenced by Ramana Maharshi and Papaji encouraged their listeners to find the source of the I-thought, or to relax into a nonjudgmental openness so as to allow the Self to shine through without obscuration. Papaji in particular was known for telling listeners to stay quiet and to be vigilant.

A newer wave mainly inspired by Wei Wu Wei and Nisargadatta Maharaj sometimes claimed to be "more nondual" and more direct. These teachers avoided recommendations and advice, arguing that giving the seeker anything to do only serves to enhance the sense of a separate self. It encourages the sense of a willing, choosing, controlling entity, which they saw as the main problem in the first place. They saw their teaching as a descriptive pointer to the truth, and not as a prescription of something to do. Though this latter group of teachers continued to use the satsang structure for their meetings, their particular slant on the teachings came to be known as "neo-advaita." Dennis discusses both these teachings.

Non-Traditional Advaita's Critique of Advaita-Vedanta

This critique is probably familiar to most readers who have attended a satsang or neo-advaitin meeting. These non-traditional forms have great respect for the nondual vision of Advaita-Vedanta; indeed, they take nondualism to be the highest teaching and ultimate truth of **all** traditional religions. ***But the traditional paths are irrelevant these days, and they take too long***, is the thought. The traditional paths, it is argued, including Advaita-Vedanta, bury the nondual truth under layers of dualistic, culturally-bound symbology and mythology. The seeker might require years of traditional teaching and mountains of foreign vocabulary words, to realize what can be seen instantly in the satsang format. Non-traditional advaita sees itself as immediate, modern, and instantly accessible – regardless of the aspirant's spiritual background.

The satsang format is very "now." It emphasizes right off the bat that one's nondual nature is the case right now, and that no time is required to become what one already is. This format uses virtually none of the tools of the traditional paths. Officially, there are no students or teachers, nothing to teach, no good works, no texts or readings, no exercises or meditations, no ethical requirements, and no time-consuming stages of psychological development or spiritual refinement. In fact, the satsang format sees the traditional tools as unnecessary baggage. Sometimes it is stated even more strongly, that the traditional methods are counterproductive, actually strengthening the core illusion that there is some place to get and someone to get there.

Advaita-Vedanta's response

Dennis's argument is this. Yes, Advaita-Vedanta agrees with non-traditional advaita that the nature of reality is nondual. But Advaita-Vedanta sees as **weaknesses** the very things that non-traditional advaita sees as its **strengths**. For example, non-traditional advaita rejects the traditional spiritual tools, and thereby hampers its own ability to get its message across. It gives itself nothing to teach **with**. The person who comes to satsang seeks peace and happiness. Yet they are often given nothing more than the statement that they are not separate, that they are already the peace that they seek. Advaita-Vedanta's articulation of the core illusion gives the seeker much more to grasp and it has a wide variety of time-tested methods for dissolving the illusion.

On behalf of Advaita-Vedanta, Dennis brings forth two principal criticisms of non-traditional advaita. One is that by denying the reality of the seeker, non-traditional teachings create a sense of confusion and despondency in the very person who has come to the teachings for help. The seeker still **feels** real, and this feeling is more powerful and meaningful than the teacher's abstract statement to the contrary. And with no tools to work with and all exits cut off by the non-traditional teacher's pronouncements, the seeker feels that there is no hope.

Dennis's other main criticism is more serious. He argues that non-traditional advaita misunderstands the nature of enlightenment. Traditionally, Advaita-Vedanta follows the scriptures and defines enlightenment as self-knowledge. This knowledge is not a feeling. It is not a statement *about* something. Self-knowledge is rather like an unmistakable, irreversible recognition. One recognizes the nondualistic identity of all existence. One recognizes that one *is* Brahman, and also that there is *only* Brahman. This recognition requires no vigilance or rehearsal. There is no going back from it.

On the other hand, the non-traditional advaita teachings have psychologized the notion of enlightenment, making it shaky and reversible. This is perhaps to be expected, since non-traditional advaita is largely a Western phenomenon. Many non-traditional teachers had been workshop leaders or psychologists before coming to the spiritual path. The dominant Western way of thinking about one's self in the twenty-first century tends to be psychological and medical. So in spite of downplaying or denying the existence of the person and saying that "everyone is already enlightened," there is still a personalistic and psychological slant to non-traditional teachings. In spite of saying that "there's no one there," many teachers still tell triumphal stories that they see as their narratives of enlightenment. The earlier satsang teachers, relying on a phrase from Papaji, tended to characterize enlightenment as the "death of the mind." This was described as a phenomenally quiet mind, a mind in which very few thoughts, if any, would appear. This quietness allows the Self to shine through without obscuration, according to the formula,

No thoughts = Self is revealed ("I'm there!")
Thoughts = Self is concealed ("I've slipped back into duality.")

The more recent neo-advaita teachers use a harder-edged terminology, often saying that "afterwards," there is still "a body/mind mechanism" present. Thoughts may arise, which needn't be few and needn't be quiet. The big difference is that certain categories of thoughts and feelings no longer arise. Or if they do arise, they are seen as the automatic functioning of the mechanism.

Both these non-traditional characterizations of enlightenment are simply psychological descriptions of a set of experiences. Such characterizations encourage seekers to constantly monitor themselves and judge their state accordingly. Following these teachings, one usually can't avoid equating *what one is* with *how one feels*. The teachings make enlightenment hostage to the momentary particularities of one's thought stream. Even **success** according to these psychological criteria is a far cry from the vast nondual vision of enlightenment according to Advaita-Vedanta.

Through a close examination of both the traditional and non-traditional teachings, Dennis shows how Advaita-Vedanta puts the tools of liberation back in place. The time-honored methods are still relevant, he argues. The tools are safe, and free from the "practice makes it worse" charge levied by the non-traditional teachings.

To my knowledge this is the first book of its kind.

Dr. Greg Goode

Introduction

I began this book as an attempt to compare and contrast the various methods of presentation of advaita in the West, believing that each would have its own merits and shortcomings. My own direct experience of the various approaches consists of around fifteen years with a school 'directed by' an Indian sage, followed by a further ten of extensive personal study and research (with several books to document the findings). This has included only a few visits to satsang and neo-advaitin teachers and my principal source of information has been reading and communication with others – teachers, writers and seekers - who have far greater personal experience of these teachers. The key point to note here is that, in the course of writing this book, the emphasis necessarily changed. I realized that it was not easy to find points of recommendation for satsang teaching and even less so for neo-advaitin satsangs, whereas their negative aspects became increasingly apparent. Even the title of the book has changed as a result of this and it is now clear that only traditional teaching can be seriously recommended; the certain dangers and potential pitfalls of non-traditional approaches are far too real. Accordingly, the aim is now to set down clearly, reasonably and unarguably the facts of the matter: what enlightenment is (and isn't) and why traditional techniques will take you there while Western-style satsang and neo-advaita are unlikely to do so.

It is also noticeable that it is sometimes (in the book) unclear whether a comment applies to satsang, neo-advaita or both. An earlier draft attempted to specify this explicitly but these flags have now been removed. The reasons for this are twofold. Firstly, the distinction between the two approaches seems to be becoming less clear as some teachers with connections to traditional sources are making statements more usually associated with neo-advaitin teachers. Secondly, neither approach can be recommended, despite the fact that what is said by many satsang teachers is correct. It is hoped that this view will be shared by anyone who reads the book with an open mind.

Key Definitions

advaita - the non-dual philosophy, based upon the Upanishads and systematized by Shankara around the 8th Century AD. The word itself means 'not two'. It is sometimes referred to as 'Advaita Vedanta'. 'Vedanta' refers to the Vedas, the ancient documents which also contain most of the Upanishads as their end portions (Sanskrit 'anta'). [But it should be noted that other philosophies also utilize the Vedas.]

enlightenment – This term is much confused and misused. It is self-ignorance that prevents recognition of the truth about our nature and that of reality. Enlightenment takes place in the mind of a person when self-ignorance has been eradicated. It is true (in absolute reality) that we are already 'free' - there is only ever the non-dual reality so how could it be otherwise? It is *not* true that we are already enlightened (in empirical reality), as the seeker well knows. Enlightenment is the event in time when the mind realizes that we are already free.

self-knowledge – It is only self-knowledge that removes self-ignorance; and that removal is termed 'enlightenment'. But it needs to be understood from the outset that this is not objective knowledge about the nature of the body and mind (which we are not), or pointers to the nature of the Self or brahman (which we are). Self-knowledge is the very specific recognition that I am already That which I have been seeking.

neo-advaita - the style of teaching that purports to express only the final, absolute truth of advaita. It does not admit of any 'levels' of reality and does not recognize the existence of a seeker, teacher, ignorance, spiritual path etc. Whereas satsang teachers in general differ quite widely as regards their particular ways of talking about and teaching advaita, neo-advaitin teachers do not. The statements of one are essentially inter-changeable with those of another, with only personal style and coined phrases differing.

satsang – in its traditional use, the word literally means 'association with the wise or good' (from the Sanskrit satsa~Nga) and refers to a group of true seekers (sAdhaka-s) led by a qualified teacher – see 131. It refers to a meeting in which some teaching is given, followed by question and answer. The word is most commonly used now in the West in the sense of 'good company', simply to refer to a group of people gathered together to discuss (advaita) philosophy. This is the sense in which it is used in this book. The fundamental difference is that satsang forms just a part of traditional teaching whereas it is the entirety of most Western teaching.

[Note that, throughout the book, passages in italics beneath a numbered point indicate additional commentary or illustration. Italicized extracts within a numbered point indicate a quotation, which is normally followed by a reference to the bibliography. Occasionally, a word is italicized for emphasis. Sanskrit words are accordingly *not* italicized. It was suggested by one reviewer that I emphasize particularly important points by **bold text**. I decided against this, since I felt it would detract from the appearance and inhibit comfortable reading. Instead, the key points have been summarized at the end of the book.]

Context

The Reader

1   As the reader of this book, you are likely to be someone who knows at least a little about advaita but wishes to learn more; someone who has attended satsangs but found that these have not provided the solid background knowledge or graduated teaching that you feel you need.

2   It is likely that you will know that you are looking for lasting happiness, fulfillment or meaning in your life. You will probably believe that you are seeking 'enlightenment' but may not be entirely sure what this is.

3   You may be a 'long-term seeker' but still not a 'finder'. You may have visited many different satsang teachers yet somehow failed to find the 'right one'.

4   You may enjoy satsangs very much and feel that meeting like-minded people in a spiritually conducive environment is very valuable. But you may also feel that you are not 'moving forward' in any sense.

5   Possibly you wonder whether this is your own fault, the fault of the teacher or their method of teaching.

6   You may be a reader of books by neo-advaitin teachers and/or you may attend their satsangs. In this case, you may feel unable to relate your own experience and understanding with the language that such teachers use, despite the fact that you may feel that what they say is 'true'.

Purpose of the Book (and Disclaimers)

7   Some of the statements in the book are likely to be contentious and

may upset some readers. Accordingly, this section should be read carefully (at least once!) so that the intentions behind the book are clearly understood.

8   The purpose is specifically to address the concerns of seekers who are dissatisfied with the satsang or neo-advaitin approaches to the teaching of advaita and to answer related questions.

9   It attempts clearly to define the principal terms which are used when discussing these matters, especially such words as 'enlightenment', 'person', teacher' etc.

10   It is not primarily a book about non-duality but about the *teaching* of non-duality. It discusses the guru and the seeker and the ways in which the former relate to the latter's attempts to become enlightened.

11   In particular, it compares and contrasts the traditional methods, passed down from teacher to student for over a thousand years with the far less formal methods adopted by modern satsang and neo-advaitin teachers.

12   The book makes no specific claims about relative 'success rates' of the different approaches. There are no statistics available upon which any such claims might be made and views might well differ even upon whether a given teacher is 'enlightened' or not. What it will do is to present, analyze and criticize the various issues and endeavor to persuade the reader that anything other than the traditional approach is unlikely to succeed.

I anticipate that the majority of readers of the book will be students of Western satsang-style teaching, possibly with an emphasis on neo-advaita. I aim to explain to these readers why they might be feeling dissatisfied with the teaching to which they are currently exposed and to suggest why traditional methods might prove more fruitful. My own position is that satsang on its own is deficient in many respects, while neo-advaita is most unlikely to be helpful to the majority of seekers.

13   It utilizes the terms of advaita because this particular philosophy is the one with which I am familiar. It is assumed that the reader is aware of the basic principles and this book will not specifically attempt to teach them. Nevertheless, terms will be defined when they are introduced and some aspects of the teaching will be explained in order to clarify the points being discussed. Brief definitions of all the terms used can be found in the *Definition of Key Terms* section at the end of the book.

For an introduction to non-duality for those who do not know what it is, see Ref. 65. For an intermediate and fairly complete treatment of advaita, see Ref. 1 and, for an advanced and detailed examination, see Ref. 2.

14   I do not want to include lots of technical detail, which may be found distracting. However, in order to provide satisfactory and reasonable explanations, it is sometimes necessary to go into some depth, including using Sanskrit words with which the reader may be unfamiliar. This only happens occasionally and it is suggested that, if you find such points too detailed, you simply ignore them and revisit them later if needed.

15   I decided to write this book in note form. Initially, this was done from a practical point of view, the better to organize my thoughts and avoid repetition. It is also, of course, the 'sutra' form of traditional scriptures and their commentaries. I may also have been influenced by Wittgenstein's style of presentation, though make no claims for an equivalent level of intellectual rigor! Additionally, however, I realized that many readers, especially those committed

to satsangs (and in particular the teachers themselves) are going to want to take issue with some of the statements. I thought it would make this easier if I numbered each of the key points.

16   I would like to emphasize that this book is not criticizing specific teachers nor suggesting that anyone is inept or unenlightened. I am criticizing satsang as a teaching method, when used on its own and attended only infrequently, as is typical in the West. Specific teachers are not usually quoted, since I did not want to imply that anyone was being singled out for disapprobation. Instead, I have endeavored to paraphrase actual quotations to make the points in a more general way. Those quotations which are present are included because they are particularly helpful and relevant to the point being made.

17   Also I am not primarily criticizing neo-advaita in respect of the truth or falsehood of its actual statements but as regards its utility as a teaching methodology. (Though the flaws in some neo-advaitin views are highlighted in passing.)

18   Whilst it is true (almost by definition) that all neo-advaitin teaching is effectively the same (and therefore demonstrably unhelpful), the same cannot be said of all satsang teaching. It is perfectly possible that some teachers will try to embody some methodology in their teaching and, in some cases, this may take due cognizance of the ideal traditional procedures and for this they must be applauded. It is, however, unfortunately true that the extent to which they will be able to do this is inevitably constrained by the satsang format itself and, even more significantly, by time.

19   Where Sanskrit words are used, these are written in ITRANS format. (This is described in the appendices of Refs. 1 & 2 and at my website http://www.advaita.org.uk/sanskrit/itrans.htm.) One aspect of Sanskrit that may cause confusion if you are not already

aware of it is that there are no capital letters. Thus, sentences beginning with a Sanskrit word will not begin with a capital, nor are any used for proper names. The capitals that are used in ITRANS indicate completely different letters in the Sanskrit alphabet, which has 49 characters in total.

20   There are two main sources of epistemological problems associated with the teaching of non-duality:

a) Confusion of absolute reality with relative reality. The former is non-dual and undifferentiated; the latter refers to the empirical world, in which teacher, seeker and path are all meaningful.

b) Failure to define the terms that are used in discussions. Accordingly, it is necessary for some preliminary explanations so that these problems may be avoided in this book. The key terms and concepts, which form the subject matter of the book, therefore have their own sections, immediately following.

advaita – Non-duality

21   Very briefly, the meaning of the word 'advaita' is 'not two'. It teaches that reality is non-dual; that the world of people and things is simply name and form of that non-dual reality (brahman). The world is said to be 'dependent' upon brahman or brahman is the 'essential nature' of the world. We mistakenly assume that these forms (including ourselves) have a separate, independent existence. This mistake is the result of self-ignorance, which occurs in the mind. With the appropriate knowledge, this ignorance can be dispelled and 'we' become enlightened.

22   The ultimate non-dual reality is referred to by many different names and not all teachers use these words for that purpose. Examples are: Absolute, Self, Consciousness, Awareness, Truth, Knowledge, Presence, Love. Whichever word is used, what usually gives it away

is the capitalization. But the safest way of avoiding misunderstanding is to stick to those terms that have been used for thousands of years in the advaita tradition, namely brahman (when speaking in general terms) or Atman (when referring to this principle in reference to an apparent 'person'). These are the terms used in this book.

23   When speaking of this non-dual truth, one has already departed from it, in that one cannot really speak about it at all.

24   In particular, a sentence which has one of the above terms (Self, Consciousness etc.) as the subject and *anything at all as the predicate* **must** be mixing up absolute and relative levels of reality. [The exception is a 'self-defining' sentence such as 'the Self is brahman'.] Thus, claims such as 'the Self has our true interests at heart' can immediately be dismissed as nonsense - 'the Self' is the non-dual reality and 'our', 'interests' etc. are part of the mistaken view of that reality. In general, any statement at all about the non-dual reality may be dismissed, although traditional advaita has useful, proven ways of using some statements as 'pointers' to the truth.

It is acknowledged that avoiding this confusion of absolute and relative realities is often very difficult and it is not impossible that I will be found guilty of it in this book! See the later section on 'Reality and Appearance' for further explanation. But the issue cannot be avoided by refusing to acknowledge that there are such levels, as neo-advaita does!

Knowledge
25   Because knowledge is fundamental to enlightenment, it is necessary to give some explanation of advaita epistemology (theory of knowledge). This will only be a brief outline – there are whole books on this subject (e.g. Ref. 17) – but the reader may still wish

to skim or miss out this whole section on first reading.

26   Many adjectives are used when we try to talk about knowledge, e.g. direct versus indirect, subjective versus objective, immediate versus mediate, intrinsic versus extrinsic, non-dual versus dual, Self versus worldly, valid versus erroneous, etc. Consequently, there is much opportunity for confusion!

27   Ignorance is a condition of the mind (specifically the buddhi or intellect) and all knowledge 'takes place' in the mind.

28   Knowledge that ultimately proves to be 'valid' or 'true' is called pramA in Sanskrit and the various means by which such valid knowledge may be obtained are called pramANa-s. Without a pramANa, nothing can be known.

29   Advaita recognizes six pramANa-s. They are (see Glossary for more detail): direct perception – pratyakSha; inference – anumAna; comparison or analogy – upamAna; non-apprehension – anupal-abdhi; postulation or supposition – arthApatti; verbal authority or evidence – shabda.

30   The rope-snake metaphor provides a clear explanation of immediate knowledge. In total darkness, there might be a nest of vipers in the middle of the path but we would not know anything about it – we would be totally ignorant. In the twilight, when we first see the object on the path, we know that there is something there but we do not know what it is. This knowledge is indefinite and we imagine the rope to be a snake. When torchlight is shone onto the object, the rope is clearly revealed and known immediately for what it is.

This rope-snake metaphor is probably the most famous in advaita scriptures and is quoted in the commentaries of gauDapAda on the mANDUkya upaniShad. Seeing the snake is an error or adhyAsa. In just such a way we superimpose the illusion of objects etc. upon the one brahman. The term 'adhyAsa' is used to refer to the "mistake" that we make when we erroneously 'superimpose' a false appearance upon the reality or mix up the real and the unreal.

[The Sanskrit term used for immediate knowledge is aparokSha. parokSha means remote, invisible or mysterious; the prefix 'a' in Sanskrit negates the word.]

31   This is effectively our starting position with respect to ourselves – we know that we exist but are ignorant of our real nature. We think that we are merely a body-mind. We are seeking that knowledge, which will reveal to us who we really are.

32   The words 'ignorance' and 'knowledge', in the context of seeking and enlightenment, always refer to self-ignorance and self-knowledge, i.e. about the nature of 'who-we-really-are'.

Direct/Indirect knowledge

33   In Vedanta, these terms simply indicate whether or not the object about which we are obtaining knowledge is available for direct perception or not. If it is present to the mind now, then any knowledge about it will be direct.

An often used example in Vedantic discussions about perception, knowledge or logic is that of seeing smoke on a distant, forested hilltop and inferring that there must be a fire. In this example, we would have direct knowledge of the hill, the forest and the smoke but our inferred knowledge about the fire would be indirect.

34   An alternative means for obtaining the knowledge about there being a fire on the hill would be for someone who we trusted to tell us that he or she has seen the fire for themselves. This means of knowledge is called shabda – verbal authority or evidence.

35 The story of the tenth man is an example of direct knowledge and a metaphor to explain how traditional teaching brings about self-knowledge or enlightenment: Ten men cross a river in flood and lose their footing. They swim to the other bank and re-assemble. When they count the number of survivors, they find only nine and lament the loss of one. A passing monk hears their story and realizes their mistake. He touches each man, counting out the number, and thus demonstrates that all ten are present. Each man, when counting the others, had forgotten to count himself. Similarly, we each forget our true self until this is pointed out by the teacher. In the context of the story, as the monk touches the last man and says 'you are the tenth', direct knowledge arises.

36 Shankara explains that statements about the Self convey direct knowledge (because the Self is actually available here and now for us to ratify such statements): *"Indirect knowledge, it is true, is the result produced by the sentences regarding the non-Self, but it is not so in the case of those regarding the Innermost Self. It is, on the other hand, direct and certain knowledge like that in the case of the tenth boy."* Upadesha Sahasri II.18.202 (Ref. 81)

37 In the case of 'worldly' knowledge, we have to apply the knowledge, once it has been obtained, in order to achieve a particular goal. With self-knowledge, the knowledge itself brings about the goal automatically – we do not have to do anything because we are *already* the non-dual Self.

38 The technique of bhAga tyAga lakShaNa is a very clear example of how a method in advaita can bring about direct knowledge. See 426.

Scriptural or Verbal Testimony (shabda)

39 Much or our knowledge is gained via our own direct perception or by inference or reasoning based upon that perception. Far more is gained through reading, watching television and so on. We do not

18

question the existence of China, for example, even though we may never have been there and have only seen it represented on a map and heard it discussed on the news.

40   Where the related knowledge is indirect, there is always the possibility that the source of the testimony is either mistaken or is intentionally misleading us. You may, for example, have seen the movie 'Capricorn One', in which NASA misled the world about a supposed mission to Mars. The launch and eventual landing were televised but in fact the spaceship had not been manned and the landing was simulated in a film studio. (Some people believe that the moon landings were faked in such a manner.)

41   Where the related knowledge is direct however, as is the case when it is about ourselves, it is not possible for us to be misled in this way.

42   shabda is unique in being able to communicate knowledge about our true nature. All other means of knowledge are only able to tell us about those things that are accessible to the senses. The brahma sUtra-s (II.i.27) state that *"But (this has to be accepted) on the authority of the Upanishads, for brahman is known from the Upanishads alone."* and Shankara adds: *"Hence a supersensuous thing is truly known from the Vedic source alone."* (Ref. 88)

43   Traditionally, the scriptures are regarded as the only source of knowledge about the Self. The author of the Brahma Sutras, bAdarAyaNa, makes this clear at the beginning of this definitive work (I.i.3): *"(Brahman is not known from any other source), since the scriptures are the valid means of Its knowledge."* (Ref. 88)

44   They approach the subject tangentially, using apparent or unreal attributes (e.g. using 'blue' to point out the sky); incidental attributes (e.g. the house with the crow sitting on the roof); absence of attributes (e.g. bring me the glass which is empty); indirection

(e.g. neti, neti – not this, not this); and implication. (Ref. 34)

45   More is said about the scriptures themselves in 116 - 128.

Self-Ignorance

46   Traditionally, the root cause of the beliefs that we are separate, that there is a dualistic world, that we are unhappy and so on is self-ignorance – avidyA.

47   Given the fact that, in reality, there is only brahman, the existence of 'self-ignorance' is not easy to explain. It would seem that either brahman or the jIva must be the locus of the ignorance but either poses problems. The post-Shankara vivaraNa school claims the former while the bhAmatI school claims the latter. The essential reason for the diverging views is the ultimate irreconcilability of absolute reality with the empirical world – a problem which will crop up again and again in this book.

Shankara states that: "We agree that the Absolute is not the author of Ignorance and that it is not deluded by it either. Even so, there is nothing other than the Absolute which is the author of Ignorance, and no other conscious being apart from the Absolute that is deluded by it." bRRihadAraNyaka upaniShad bhAShya I.iv.10 (quoted in Ref. 27) *And in his brahma sUtra bhAShya (I.4.3), he says that brahman is the Ashraya of avidyA. It is probably in respect of the word 'Ashraya' that the differences of opinion arise. Most of Shankara's disciples translate it as 'locus' but the bhAmatI school translate it as 'content'. (Ref. 101)*

48   The bhAmatI-s attribute two aspects to avidyA: a 'veiling power', called AvaraNa (which prevents us from seeing the reality of the rope, in the rope-snake metaphor) and a 'projecting power', called vikShepa (which projects the appearance of the snake). Our experience is already non-dual; we already are brahman but the fact

is covered over by AvaraNa, allowing the mistaken mind to project the illusion of duality.

49   Only self-knowledge can dispel self-ignorance.

50   The self-ignorance is in the mind. The appropriate use of the means of self-knowledge (i.e. presented according to proven, traditional methods by a skilled teacher to a prepared and receptive mind) *automatically* removes the ignorance.

But receipt of unsupported statements, without any method (e.g. the bare statement that 'This is it') is effectively only adding more ignorance about the nature of the self and reality to that which is already there.

51   In truth, we are already the Self; it is the mind that thinks otherwise.

52   Consequently, 'enlightenment' is that 'event' in the mind that dissolves this self-ignorance once and for all.

"By mind alone can That (brahman) be attained, There is no difference between the two (brahman and the world). He who sees them as different goes from death to death." Katha Upanishad II.1.11 (Ref. 93)

53   Since it occurs in the mind of the person, it *does* make sense to say that it is the person who becomes enlightened.

54   Once self-ignorance is admitted as the problem, then it follows necessarily that self-knowledge is required to remove it. In turn this implies the need for a teacher or material to impart that knowledge and consequently, effectively a path and a seeker etc. We do not have any sense organ for 'self-knowledge'. All of the usual pramANa-s only provide information about the world of facts,

observations and information (which includes our body and the subtle aspects of thoughts and emotions); i.e. all of the senses 'turn outwards' as the quotation below indicates. The only pramANa for knowledge about our true Self is shabda.

The Katha Upanishad, II.1.1 says: "Death said: 'God made sense turn outward, man therefore looks outward, not into himself. Now and again a daring soul, desiring immortality, has looked back and found himself.'" (Ref. 90)

55   Once the self-ignorance has been removed, there is no return according to traditional teaching. Satsang teaching often implies that vigilance is needed to ensure that identification with the non-self (ahaMkAra) does not return. Genuine self-knowledge is, however, irrevocable. [See 110 for an explanation of ahaMkAra.]

56   Neo-advaitins deny the existence of a seeker and of enlightenment and the possibility of a path leading to it. They deny that Self-ignorance is the cause of our problems and Self-knowledge the solution to it.

57   Since all of these are in the realm of duality and advaita tells us that reality is non-dual, it is indeed a paradox. Shankara acknowledges this paradox – see the quotation in 47.

Self-knowledge

58   All 'worldly' knowledge refers to supposedly separate things, ideas etc. in the apparent world. Such knowledge is usually indirect and subject to revision in the light of new experience. Science deals in this kind of knowledge. It is necessarily dualistic, being perceived by a 'subject'.

59   Self-knowledge is quite different. It refers to our true self. When it takes place, it is direct and immediate. It is not subject to revision.

It has always been the case (simply 'covered over' by ignorance) and will always remain so. It is not that something is gained, rather that the self-ignorance is removed.

60   The scriptures point out that such knowledge cannot be taught: "*The eye does not go there, nor speech, nor mind. We do not know That. We do not know how to instruct one about It. It is distinct from the known and above the unknown.*" Kena Upanishad I.3 (Ref. 85) But Shankara's commentary on this verse states that: "*True it is that one cannot impart knowledge about the Highest with the help of such means of valid knowledge as the evidence of the senses; but the knowledge can be produced with the help of traditional authority.*" (Ref. 86)

61   Knowing that 'I am brahman' is not really the normal usage of the word 'know', which in all other cases implies a dualistic knower-subject and known-object. 'I am brahman' is direct self-knowledge. The guru is able to utilize the words and methods of shabda pramANa in order to enable this process in the seeker.

62   Knowledge about oneself, subjective knowledge or 'Self-knowledge', could be regarded as a synonym for 'enlightenment'.

63   The knowledge acquired when the scriptures are 'unfolded' by a qualified teacher is immediate. 'Qualified' means one who is Self-realized (a brahmaniShTha), who understands the scriptures (a shrotriya) and who knows how to use them as a means of self-knowledge. Thus it is that, as a seeker is taught by a traditional teacher, self-knowledge grows (or, it might be said, knowledge 'vRRitti-s' [mental dispositions] are acquired). The final 'knowledge vRRitti' – the akhaNDAkAra vRRitti [akhaNDAkAra means 'form of the undivided'] – brings enlightenment (see 99).

64   This knowledge is imparted by the use of proven techniques, which

will be described later (see 419 - 431) but, as an example, Shankara says in his treatise (vAkya vRRitti) on the mahAvAkya [aphorism] 'tattvamasi' [That thou art]: *"Direct knowledge of that total identity between the individual-Self and the Universal-Self, stemming forth from the Vedic statements such as "Thou art that", etc., is the immediate means to liberation."* (Ref. 89) [tattvamasi is possibly the most well-known of the four principal 'great sayings' (mahAvAkya-s) from the Upanishads and is translated: 'thou art That' – tvam means 'you' singular; asi means 'are'; tat means 'That', i.e. brahman.]

65   It is likely that any knowledge gained by simply reading the scriptures will remain at the level of information (probably misunderstood and certainly not assimilated), since there is no accompanying explanation by a qualified teacher who is also aware of our current level of understanding.

shravaNa, manana and nididhyAsana

66   Listening to a suitably qualified teacher is the first step of the key method in traditional teaching – shravaNa, manana and nididhyAsana. shravaNa means simply listening to the words; manana means reflecting on those words, questioning the teacher and clarifying one's understanding through discussion; nididhyAsana means meditating upon that which was understood at the time of the actual teaching.

67   There are differing views upon which aspect of this process is the actual 'cause' of self-knowledge. The candidates for the causality are: hearing the scriptures (shravaNa), subsequent meditation upon what has been heard (nididhyAsana) or the mind of the student herself.

68   There were a number of conflicting views prior to and around the time of Shankara and he spent much of his short life consolidating

his own stance and systematically rejecting contradictory positions. After his death, commentaries were written on Shankara's commentaries on the Upanishads and Brahmasutras and further commentaries written on those so that divergent interpretations soon began to form.

69 Two specific, influential branches of advaita have differing views on a number of topics. In this context the vivaraNa School believes that hearing a sentence alone can produce direct knowledge in the case where the purport of the sentence is something that is itself immediately known (aparokSha). vivaraNa therefore emphasizes the primacy of shravaNa, although they consider shravaNa, manana and nididhyAsana to be an integral process rather than separate steps.

70 The bhAmatI School, on the other hand, believes that a sentence on its own can only give indirect knowledge. Therefore, after hearing the words, the direct knowledge must be intuitively realized by the mind as a result of nididhyAsana.

"The self is not grasped by eyes or words, nor perceived by the senses nor revealed by rituals and penance. When the understanding becomes calm and refined, then in meditation, one realizes Him, the Absolute." Mundaka Upanishad III.1.8 (Ref. 100)

71 In the vivaraNa School, hearing the great aphorisms, such as tat tvam asi is regarded as the direct cause of enlightenment and the guru lineage is extremely important. This school is considered to most nearly align with the views and intentions of Shankara and thus best represents the 'traditional' approach.

Shankara states in the upadeSha sAhasrI (18.103): "The listening to the teaching and the production of right knowledge are simultaneous, and the result is the cessation of (the transmigratory existence consisting of) hunger etc. There can be no doubt about the meaning of the sentences like 'Thou art That' in the past, present or future." (Ref. 81) The 'tenth man' story is given as an example of how this works – see 35.

72   The bhAmatI school believe that the process is a stepwise rather than an integral one and they say that the guru is needed only for shravaNa and manana; it is the subsequent concentrated meditation by the student alone which brings enlightenment. These views have gained prominence in recent times as a result of the teaching of Vivekananda and are those expressed throughout the Ramakrishna and Vivekananda organizations. Traditional advaitins have called such teachings 'neo-Vedanta' (not to be confused with neo-advaita).

73   A. J. Alston, in his six-volume compilation of Shankara's teaching says that: *"Shankara's solution of this apparent impasse is to prescribe repetition of the whole discipline of hearing, reflection and sustained meditation until, through the gradual shedding of all misconceptions, there comes a time when the hearer attains to immediate intuition on hearing the text for the last time."* (Ref. 91) (Obviously 'solution' is the wrong word here, since the dispute did not begin until after his death!)

74   As indicated, the preferred, traditional explanation is that liberating 'knowledge vRRitti-s' occur in the mind of the seeker as the words of the teacher are heard. The traditional teaching literally takes us to the goal.

This is illustrated by the following metaphor of a road-map. If I want to drive from A to B, I might well make use of a map. Initially, I will simply look at the map, noting the relative positions of A and B and the roads that join them. Indeed, in my mind, I might actually follow the route on the map that I need to take. But this will not get me to B. I actually need to drive the car along the physical roads.

26

This is not how the scriptures function as a pramANa. The scriptures function as the actual road that the mind needs to take. The guru acts as the guide, having already travelled the road previously. The journey is not metaphorical. If we follow the scriptural route, using our reason, referring to our own experience and asking the guru for clarification when necessary, it will lead us to the goal of self-knowledge.

Teaching advaita

75   There are two complementary aspects to the traditional teaching of advaita. Firstly, the 'negating aspect' of traditional teaching aims to remove our misconceptions about the nature of the world and ourselves. Secondly, the 'positive aspect' utilizes metaphor and other techniques to point towards our real nature.

76   An alternative way of looking at this is that the 'neti, neti' injunction neutralizes the vikShepa aspect of avidyA (the identification with body and mind etc.), while the pointers to our real nature as brahman counteracts the AvaraNa aspect.

Viewed in this way, advaita might be regarded as the torch that is shone on the rope-snake. Its light dispels (i.e. negates) the illusory, projected snake and reveals (i.e. points to the reality of) the reality of the rope.

77   The reason for this is simply that the non-dual reality cannot be described by language, as the Taittiriya Upanishad (II.ix.1) points out: "*The enlightened man is not afraid of anything after realising that bliss of brahman, **failing to reach which, words turn back along with the mind**.*" (Ref. 102)

78   Thus, the scriptures provide negative expressions such as: Brihadaranyaka Upanishad II.v.19: "*...it is brahman who has not a before nor an after, nor a beside, nor a without...*" (Ref. 103) and

later (III.viii.8) it uses words such as akShara – imperishable; asthUla – not gross; anaNu – not minute; ahrasva – not short; adIrgha – not long; anantara – has no inside; abhAya – has no outside and so on.

79 And they provide positive indications of its essential nature (svarUpa lakShaNa): Taittiriya Upanishad (II.i.1) *"brahman is truth, knowledge, and infinite"* (Ref. 102). And, from the Mandukya Upanishad (verse 7): shAntaM shivamadvaitaM – the non-dual, peaceful and blissful.

80 But the principal method is to point to those aspects that differentiate it from the apparently existing things in the empirical world, i.e. extrinsic rather than intrinsic properties. e.g. Taittiriya Upanishad III.i.1:

'That' from whence all beings are born,
'That' by which, when born, they live,
'That' into which they enter at death
'That' is brahman
(Ref. 104)
Other examples are those from the Kena Upanishad – see 60 and 401.

81 The ultimate realization that is gained from advaita is 'absolute', i.e. it is not subject to later correction, revision, or qualification as is the case with scientific knowledge. Nor can it be sublated. [Sublation or bAdha can be thought of as a 'paradigm shift', when a particular way of looking at something changes completely, just as when the desert oasis is realized to be a mirage.]

82 Without appropriate preparation and teaching, the mind of the student is rarely able fully to accept and appreciate non-dual philosophy.

83   The belief in oneself as a separate 'person' (with a body, mind, sense organs, roles, opinions etc.) is extremely tenacious. It is necessary to separate out the 'I' that is identifying with all of these things. When they have all been negated, what remains is who I really am.

Traditional teaching provides many pointers and scriptural 'explanation' to help the mind to appreciate the nature of this 'essential I'. Neo-advaitin and satsang approaches may be good at the negating process but are very poor at the positive aspect of clarification.

84   Consequently, even if what is stated by satsang teachers is 'correct', it is unlikely genuinely to be assimilated.

85   Many satsang teachers imply that enlightenment has nothing to do with gaining any sort of knowledge but is simply being in the present and accepting that you already are that for which you are searching.

86   According to the traditional teachings however, we cannot see that we are already free because of avidyA. The explanations provided by traditional teaching enable direct recognition of the Self that we already are. Lacking this, we will simply continue in our state of self-ignorance, identifying with body and mind. Simply 'being present' for the 'unenlightened' means living with the misunderstanding and the consequent suffering and this definitely does not seem like liberation.

87   To some degree, it is that very suffering that drives one to seek the truth and to that extent, it is actually valuable. Simply 'dropping' the suffering, even assuming that were possible, would not achieve the desired end.

88   The 'enlightenment' comes, not when the suffering is dropped but

when the mind ultimately takes on the form of the truth, and then the self-ignorance that was the cause of the suffering disappears spontaneously.

Goal of teaching

89 The ultimate goal of the teaching is, of course, to bring about enlightenment in the mind of the seeker. This may be perceived by a particular seeker as being a gradual process or a sudden one or even as a gradual series of sudden insights. Various metaphors might be used to illustrate this as follows.

90 Swami Parthasarathy has given the metaphor of using Brasso (a commercial metal cleaner) to clean a brass ornament. Initially the ornament may appear entirely blackened and the 'truth' of the brass is completely hidden. But, as you apply the work of rubbing with the Brasso (practice, shravaNa etc.), the hidden luster of the metal starts to be revealed until, when all of the tarnish and grime (Self-ignorance) has been removed, the gleaming Self is revealed as having been there all the time. The truth about the Self is directly revealed as the related ignorance is removed just as the underlying brass is directly seen as the tarnish is wiped away.

91 Similar to this is that of fog slowly lifting to reveal the landscape or a Polaroid photograph gradually developing. In each case, the scene is initially not visible at all, then partially. Only ultimately is it revealed in all its clarity.

92 The metaphor of switching on the lights in a dark room is the other extreme, going from complete ignorance to total knowledge in an instant. This is an extremely unlikely event but not inconceivable.

93 Intermediate between the two might be switching on a succession of spotlights. As one bit of teaching is given, understanding dawns and pieces of the overall 'landscape' of reality are permanently illumi-

nated. When all of the spotlights have finally been turned on, all is clearly seen. With this metaphor, it could be said that enlightenment proceeds by sudden jumps but might be considered to be gradual overall.

94   It should be noted that, whatever the process might be, it is the removal of self-ignorance that is gradual or sudden; enlightenment itself is binary – we either are or are not enlightened.

Ramana Maharshi says: "Self realization itself does not admit of progress, it is ever the same. The Self remains always in realization. The obstacles are thoughts. Progress is measured by the degree of removal of the obstacles to understanding that the Self is always realized." (Ref. 28) I.e. it is not possible to be 'partly' enlightened – you either are or you are not – but the removal of ignorance is necessarily gradual.

95   **akhaNDAkAra vRRitti:** whichever of the various views best describes the overall process, this final 'knowledge vRRitti' (see 99) is said to produce a quantum leap in understanding. It is not that dawning knowledge enables one subsequently to see the truth – the truth instantaneously dissolves the ignorance. This vRRitti could be said to 'catapult' the seeker into complete self-knowledge. (The vRRitti-s also disappears immediately since there is no longer the duality of knower and known.)

96   It could also be said that there are two 'parts' to enlightenment, relating to the two fundamental truths revealed by the scriptures:
a) that I am brahman;
b) that there is *only* brahman.

97   They are, of course, not unrelated but the full and final realization is of both 'aspects'. Then, self-knowledge is complete; this is called j~nAna niShThA - the knowledge that this Self is all that there is.

Enlightenment

98   This has effectively been defined above as the event in the mind that removes Self-ignorance. Much more will be said later about what enlightenment is and what it is not but here is a more formal, traditional definition:

99   "Knowledge has to come only in the locus of ignorance. Ignorance is present in the False Self, also called jIva. In Vedantic terminology this is called the antaHkaraNa where the reflection of the Real Self, Pure Consciousness, is available. It is this admixture of the antaHkaraNa (mind) and the Pure Consciousness that is called jIva. This is the false self. It is this jIva that experiences Self-ignorance and saMsAra (the 'eternal cycle' of birth and death). It is this jIva that strives for knowledge. Ultimately it is this jIva that gets the Realization. It happens through a peculiar vRRitti (transformation of the mind) called akhaNDAkAra vRRitti. When due to prolonged practice, the mind takes on the form of brahman, there occurs the destruction of the ignorance located in the jIva and thereby the jIva gets liberated. Once this happens, that person is no longer jIva but brahman.

"If the above explanation is too complicated, just this much would suffice: It is the False Self that gets the realization. This marks the end of the 'false' and just the 'Self' remains." (Ref. 23)

100   The neo-advaitin claims that 'we are already enlightened'. This is a fundamental error, which results from a failure to define terms clearly, and causes much confusion. It is true that we are already brahman, the non-dual reality, because there is only That. The point is that we do not realize this. Enlightenment takes place when we do. This is why the term Self-realization is also used – it is the direct knowing of the Self that we already are.

101   The error may well arise from the use of the Sanskrit term mokSha

for enlightenment. Strictly speaking the word means 'liberation', which is misleading because we are already 'free' in reality. What it refers to is liberation from the mistaken belief that we are **not** free.

Experience

102   Experience alone is insufficient to remove self-ignorance and can, indeed, appear to contradict self-knowledge. A metaphor for this would be the sun still appearing to go round the earth, despite the fact that we know the contrary to be the case.

103   Any experience has a beginning and an end in time... including the 'non-dual experiences' of samAdhi (note that experiences of being intensely alive and in the present are *not* non-dual experiences).

*Even samAdhi experiences (in which there is no subject-object differentiation), although they may be useful pointers towards the ultimate truth and help to refine the mind, are **only** experiences and come to an end.*

104   The function of traditional teaching, and use of the scriptures, is not to provide any experience - we already have the non-dual experience in deep sleep. (Indeed we have it all the time but we confuse the real with the unreal as noted in 166 onwards.) Instead their aim is to correct the wrong conclusion we have made on the basis of our experiences, namely that we are affected and limited by the changing experiences of the body-mind.

We are no more affected by experiences than the space is affected by the pot that appears to delineate a 'pot space' inside it.

The 'person'

105   The word 'person' is used in this book in its *misunderstood* sense. It derives from the Latin word 'persona', which was the megaphone-mask worn by actors in the theatre to make themselves

heard by the audience. It refers to all of those roles and attitudes with which the mind identifies (see 110) – we think we are a mother or father, brother, teacher etc; we believe we are lazy, clever and funny etc. All of these characteristics make up 'who we think we are' but in fact we are none of those things. These are all attributes of body or mind, whereas we are the essential 'I' that is mistakenly identified with these. Nevertheless, it is a commonly accepted term in everyday life so will continue to be used as such in this book.

106 In reality 'we' are already brahman, simply because brahman is all there is but 'we' think that we are separate 'persons'.

107 Subsequent to enlightenment, that 'person' is known not to exist as a separate entity at all; it is known that 'I am That (i.e. brahman)'.

108 Consequently, statements such as 'there is no person to become enlightened' are willfully ignoring the context in which these terms are used. At the level of empirical reality, which is all that the seeker initially knows, there is most definitively a person to become enlightened.

109 That which is most essentially 'me', who I refer to as 'I' without any qualification, is not a person; it is the Atman, which is also brahman. This is the fact revealed by enlightenment. Until such realization, the belief in a separate entity/person remains and need not cause any problem (linguistically, that is!) (Post-realization, there is obviously no problem in using the word since there is no longer any confusion.)

Ego

110 The word 'ego' is often used in spiritual discussions and is usually construed in a negative way. Some seekers believe that the goal of their search is to 'destroy' the ego. Some teachers may even use the word to criticize (or even humiliate) the seeker. To avoid difficulties

of this nature, the word that we should normally use is the Sanskrit term ahaMkAra. Literally, this means the making (kAra) of the utterance 'I' (aham) – this is effectively the equivalent of the ego but specifically refers to the identification or attachment of our true Self with something else as noted in 105. It is considered to be an aspect of the mind in classical advaita. Therefore, whenever the word 'ego' is used in the book, it should be understood in this special sense.

It should also be appreciated that the ego actually **is** *you – since there is only the non-dual brahman, what else could it be? The point is that brahman is not the ego. A metaphor that is often used to illustrate this is that the ring is gold but gold is not the ring (the ring is simply a particular name and form of gold).*

111   Most satsang teachers and their students expect to gain a spurious spiritual detachment and gauge success according to the presence or absence of egoistic thoughts rather than any real understanding.

112   The mistaken identification of ahaMkAra is addressed by using reason to differentiate between the witness, who does not change, and all the other things that do; e.g. the body grows older and weaker, the mind becomes less incisive and the memory fails, and so on. 'I' see all this, yet remain the same.

As Atmananda Krishna Menon points out, the ego doesn't obstruct understanding, which will eventually remove it: "However much you may try to kill the ego, it will only become stronger. So you have to approach it from the other end. Everybody understands in spite of the ego. The truth is that the ego automatically dies when you understand anything. You will never succeed in bringing in light, if you insist upon removing all the darkness from your room before you do so. Therefore simply ignore the ego and try to understand, and the understanding itself will remove the ego." (Note 847 – Ref 5)

113 Similarly, the mind does not have to be literally destroyed in order to become enlightened – if it were so, how would the j~nAnI [one who knows the truth, i.e. someone who is 'realized'] subsequently function in the world? What is required is that it be metaphorically destroyed by self-knowledge. This is achieved by realizing that the mind is mithyA and does not have a separate existence.

The word 'mithyA' is an important one in traditional advaita and must be clearly understood (it will be used frequently in this book). Applied to every 'thing' in the world, it means that the object referred to is neither absolutely real (satyam) nor totally illusory (prAtibhAsika). It is so-called 'dependent' reality, i.e. it is only name and form of the non-dual brahman, which is the only true reality in the final analysis. A metaphor that is often used is that of clay and pot. The pot is ultimately only name and form of clay. There is no part of the pot that is other than clay. And yet, the pot is clearly functional – it can be used as a container for water, for example. So the pot is not exactly real, since it is just name and form of clay. But neither is it totally unreal. It is said to be neither real nor unreal, but mithyA – dependent for its ultimate reality on the clay.

114 The Atman is the satyam content of the mithyA mind. We figuratively destroy the mind by knowing Atman in the same way as we figuratively destroy the misperceived snake by realizing that it is a rope or as we destroy the dreamer by coming to know the waker. This is effectively another definition of enlightenment, entirely analogous to 'waking up'.

115 The mind is actually not destroyed by enlightenment at all but strengthened, becoming more peaceful, refined, fearless etc, although the degree to which this is achieved is dependent upon the extent of preparation that took place beforehand (sAdhana chatuShTaya sampatti – see 340).

Scriptures

116 Traditionally, 'scriptures' refer to the prasthAna traya - the three sources containing pointers to Self-knowledge:

a) shruti (refers to the Vedas, which incorporate the Upanishads), the teaching traditionally passed on by word of mouth for thousands of years

b) smRRiti (refers principally to the Bhagavad Gita) and

c) nyAya prasthAna (logical and inferential material based upon the Vedas, of which the most well known are the brahmasUtra-s).

117 According to the scriptural tradition, in order to discover the Self (i.e. become enlightened), one should first understand that nothing is to be gained from the world – objects and experiences will never bring lasting happiness because they are always changing. This is understood as a result of developing such faculties as discrimination (viveka) and detachment (vairAgya). Once this understanding has been reached, the natural progression is to want to search for true meaning and purpose, i.e. one becomes a seeker looking for enlightenment – a mumukShu. Then one seeks out a teacher. These 'mental preparations' must be carried out to some degree (see 341) in order that the subsequent teaching may be appreciated, although the methods of traditional teaching will themselves also help develop these mental qualities. (N.B. Note 228 – that it is ultimately discovered that there is no meaning/purpose to life but, by then, this discovery does not cause any problem.)

118 Neither satsang nor neo-advaitin teachers will usually refer to scriptures in any form or at any time. Satsang teachers may quote from Ramana Maharshi or Nisargadatta or from their disciples. Neo-advaitin teachers do not usually quote from anyone else ('there are no others').

119 It must be admitted and acknowledged that a skilled teacher, who is able to use the scriptures as a pramANa, is what is needed. The

words themselves do not have any magical properties. Consequently, quoting the scriptures alone will not achieve anything. (The exceptions to this are the key mahAvAkya-s, which are able to give direct knowledge in one who is prepared – see 64.)

120 The scriptures are claimed to have no value by neo-advaitin teachers. (Satsang teachers in general often also hold this view.)

Such teachers have probably not read them and will certainly not have understood them. As noted above, the scriptures truly are of no value if you do not know how to use them.

121 The neo-advaitin argument is that: since there is no one to become enlightened and the Self is already free, it follows that the scriptures cannot serve any useful function.

According to this argument, it must also follow that teaching of any sort is also of no value, including that of neo-advaita.

123 This objection is addressed by Shankara (or one of his successors – the authorship is disputed) in the dRRigdRRishya viveka (verse 17): *"The character of an embodied self appears through false superimposition in the sAkShin [witness] also. With the disappearance of the veiling power, the distinction (between the seer and the object) becomes clear and with it the jIva character of the sAkShin disappears."* I.e. the intellect confuses the real Self with the unreal body-mind and the scriptures provide the knowledge to remove this ignorance, thereby bringing about the realization that the Self is ever free. (Ref. 62)

[dRRigdRRishya viveka means 'discrimination between the seer and the seen – see 423.]

123 We have direct knowledge of the Self (I know that I exist) but, as a

result of adhyAsa, I believe that I am limited - a body, a scientist, unhappy etc. When the teaching has removed the superimposed, false beliefs, it is then possible to know that I am the unlimited, non-dual brahman.

A similar view is expressed in the Yoga Vasishtha, where it is pointed out by analogy that simply looking at the sky will never bring about the realization that it is not blue. "If one does not study this scripture, true knowledge does not arise in him even in millions of years." (Ref. 59)

124 Tradition does not regard the scriptures as an absolute truth that cannot be repudiated. They are treated as a reliable source of self-knowledge in which one can trust until such time as the truth is realized for oneself, at which time they are discarded along with the ignorance they helped to dispel (c.f. the metaphor of the boat to cross the river or the pole in pole vaulting – see 415). Their value is clearly indicated by the sample techniques given in this book. Since our failure directly to perceive the truth is due to ignorance, it is possible for scriptures to provide the means for that knowledge which will dispel self-ignorance and thus bring about enlightenment. In fact, scriptures are regarded as the ultimate authority if it is necessary to resolve any conflict. (And they are not 'discarded' in a literal sense of course but referred to subsequently purely for enjoyment, if not to use for teaching others.)

125 Even the most revered sages do not blindly accept the scriptures. Gaudapada, the teacher of Shankara's teacher states in his commentary (kArikA) on the Mandukya Upanishad (III.23), on the subject of the scriptures' various descriptions of creation: *"(The passing into birth may be real or illusory. Both these views are mentioned equally in the shruti.)That which is supported by shruti and corroborated by reason is alone true and not the other."* (Ref. 61)

126 Timothy Conway points out that Sages such as Ramana Maharshi also study the scriptures after realization. He says that: *"All this study promotes a balanced understanding of the various subtly nuanced teachings about authentic spiritual realization, the avoidance of common pitfalls, working through more insidious forms of delusion and attachment, and so forth."* (Ref. 80) As pointed out elsewhere, enlightenment on its own does not qualify someone to teach. The scriptures provide the necessary support to enable one to speak meaningfully to others about one's direct understanding.

127 We can never see our own face without the aid of a mirror, no matter how keen our eyesight may be. Similarly, the scriptures, together with a teacher who can interpret them, function as a mirror to enable us to 'see' the Self.

128 It is only when the scriptures have had the intended effect that they effectively become of no further utility. Ramana Maharshi puts it thus: *"The sacred lore is voluminous, different parts of it being adapted to the needs of different kinds of seekers; each seeker successively transcends portion after portion of it; that which he transcends then becomes for him useless and even false; ultimately he transcends the whole of it."* (Ref. 31) Irrespective of the truth of this, a traditional teacher will continue to respect the scriptures, just as he will continue to respect his teacher, even knowing that both are in the realm of mithyA.

It should also be noted that Ramana was not, strictly speaking, a traditional teacher in that he did not belong to a sampradAya – see 134.

The Disciple or Seeker

129 Traditionally, the seeker or sAdhaka is one who is committed to discovering his or her true nature. The expression "head in the

tiger's mouth" has been used to indicate that this is an irrevocable decision.

130 Once a teacher has been found, the seeker becomes a disciple or shiShya. The commitment should not be made lightly since part of the process involves the teacher's learning the student's idiosyncrasies and particular problems of understanding so as to be able to provide the appropriate help.

The guru

131 There are three requirements for the 'ideal' teacher:
a) they should be enlightened - a brahmaniShTha (one who is 'absorbed in and contemplating brahman');
b) they should fully understand the scriptures and their use as a means of knowledge (i.e. they should be a shrotriya) and
c) they should be a skilled teacher.

132 Any potential guru may have one or more of these requirements. Clearly one who directly knows the truth is going to be able to interpret the scriptures through their own experience rather than simply in a pedantically correct form. And, when questions are asked for clarity, someone who is enlightened may be able to give an answer directly (dependent upon their skill as a teacher, which has nothing to do with their status as enlightened.)

133 But, if you cannot find a teacher with all three qualifications, there are two points that should be borne in mind:
(i) A brahmaniShTha cannot bring about enlightenment in the seeker without using words (see 260 and 502).
(ii) It is self-knowledge, in the form of vRRitti-s – see 63, which remove the critical self-ignorance.

134 It follows from both of these that someone who is not enlightened could, through skilful use of the appropriate words, bring about

direct self-knowledge on the part of the seeker. Shankara's advice is that, if one meets someone who is enlightened but does not have the knowledge of the teaching methods passed down through the sampradAya, one may seek his blessing but should not ask for his guidance.

In the past, disciples lived with the teacher and the scriptures were unfolded to them as an intrinsic part of their way of life so that they understood exactly what was being taught. They later became teachers themselves and the tradition continued – this is the meaning of the term sampradAya, e.g. Nisargadatta Maharaj belonged to the Navnath sampradAya. Any teaching deviating from this was unlikely to survive because the authenticity was lacking. Swami Paramarthananda defines a 'competent' teacher as 'one who was a competent disciple'!

135 In conjunction with this idea, the 'Self' does not 'authorize' someone to become a teacher and the 'right answer' to a seeker's question does not simply arise automatically in one who is enlightened. Knowing the truth and being able to communicate it are not the same things.

136 Someone who is Self-realized but who does not have any Advaitic 'teaching qualifications' is referred to as a 'mystic' rather than a 'teacher' in traditional advaita.

It must be noted that there have been examples of such beings who, despite their lack of formal training or of belonging to a sampradAya, have nevertheless functioned in life as excellent teachers and left a legacy of valuable material, whether written down by themselves or by their disciples. Ramana Maharshi is an obvious example. This, however, should not be thought to detract from the general principle.

Traditional Teaching

137 'Traditional' teaching relates to those methods of 'unfolding' the scriptures (i.e. explaining their meaning in a formal, graduated manner), which have been passed on from teacher to disciple (guru-shiShya paramparA) for over a thousand years.

138 These methods utilize reason and logic (though this does not always correspond with traditional Western logic). The philosopher most responsible for systematizing the teachings was Adi Shankara, who lived around the 8th century AD. Formal paramparA (lineages) effectively trace their line back to Shankara himself. Present day organizations that utilize these methods are principally to be found in India but there are examples in the West such as those founded by Swami Chinmayananda and Swami Dayananda and *The Philosophy Foundation* in Waltham, Massachusetts.

139 In India, the maTha-s (temples/monasteries) established by Shankara continue to the present day. The shaMkarAchArya-s (AchArya means 'spiritual guide or teacher') who head these organizations still maintain the traditions of asceticism – celibacy, living on alms, an itinerant lifestyle – and continuation of the lineage is of paramount importance. (Ref. 84)

140 It is Shankara who is primarily responsible for the principles of traditional Advaita which are based upon the systematic analysis of the prasthAna traya, although the message of advaita was always present in the Upanishads.

The dating of the Upanishads is uncertain but the oldest are thought to be around 800 BCE.

141 Ideally, the seeker should have a deep and lasting commitment to one teacher. The advantage of this is that formal tuition (using the time tested methodology) can be given, so as to establish a funda-

mental understanding of advaita, as well as addressing individual problems.

142 The methodology is more important than the scriptures and a true teacher can lead the mind of the student step by step to the direct recognition of the non-dual Self without the text and without Sanskrit.

143 It is this methodology that is totally lacking in neo-advaita and usually in all non-traditional satsangs.

Satsang Teaching

144 The word derives from the Sanskrit sa~Nga (association with) and sat (the wise or good); sat also means a 'wise man' or 'sage'. The tradition was that a disciple sought out the sage and then devoted the rest of his or her life to serving the sage in exchange for the 'grace' of their teaching.

145 Satsang forms a natural part of this tradition. Typically, the teacher will take a verse from the scriptures (probably as part of a series of talks on a complete text) and will explain the meaning of this, using other examples from the scriptures together with metaphors and examples from the students' own experience. This occupies most of the session and this is then followed by questions, in which the students seek clarification for any aspect that they have not fully understood. It is this latter Q & A session that is referred to as 'satsang'.

146 These doubts and misunderstanding arise because of our pre-existing beliefs and opinions.

Opinions are usually formed automatically from parents, teachers, advertising, society, religion and culture etc. More often than not, they are negative opinions about oneself. They form part of the Self-

ignorance that obscures the realization of our true nature. They also point to an idealized vision of how we would like things to be rather than an acceptance of the way things are. Ideally, a student should associate directly with the teacher over a long period and not simply attend occasional meetings, so that all of these wrong views may be questioned and resolved. (Refs. 30 and 71)

147 The modern, Western connotation of this term is considerably different and does not really qualify as satsang in the true sense at all. The teacher may begin with introductory remarks on a particular topic (the nature of which the seeker rarely knows in advance) but this lasts only a short time and is followed by questions and answers on any topic at all, usually quite unrelated to the initial speech.

148 Satsang teaching has been around in its modern Western form for only a short time.

It can probably be considered to have originated with Sri Poonja and Nisargadatta Maharaj (the latter began to hold regular meetings around 1915) but the practice has mushroomed in the past 30 years. This compares to the thousands of years for which traditional, sampradAya teaching has been around.

149 Sri Poonja held satsangs in Lucknow in India regularly for many years and many Western seekers visited him there. Though perhaps only staying for a relatively short time, some returned to the West believing that they too were now qualified to hold satsangs themselves.

150 Modern teachers will rarely claim a lineage stretching back earlier than Ramana Maharshi or Nisargadatta Maharaj and neo-advaitin teachers invariably claim to be 'independent' of particular teachers (though many will have spent years seeking and visiting other teachers prior to their presumed realization). Neo-advaitins usually

cite their own experience as sufficient authority (they claim that what they do is not 'teaching', in any case).

151 Satsang has come to be regarded by Westerners as though it, alone, were an adequate means for achieving self-realization.

Direct Path

152 'Direct Path' advaita is a relatively new approach. It is mentioned for completeness and so that those who are familiar with it will not think that it has been overlooked. The term itself may have been coined by Ramana Maharshi but the 'method' itself gained prominence with Atmananda Krishna Menon and is now most associated with Jean Klein, Francis Lucille, Ananda Wood and Greg Goode.

153 It begins by starting with one's own experience, and tests one's assumptions against the simplicity of this experience in the moment. It examines the world, body and mind, showing through one's experience how they are nothing other than the awareness, which is the Self.

154 The direct-path approach is characterized by an uncompromising, logical approach to the truth, and in its purest form – namely the teaching of Sri Atmananda – it is most suitable for those of a philosophical bent. He gives the following description: *"vichAra-mArga (the direct path) is removal of untruth by arguments, leaving over the Truth absolute as the real Self."* (Ref. 5)

155 It differs from neo-advaita in that all of its teachings begin from the present evidence of one's experience, and its statements are backed by rigorous logic. Whereas a neo-advaita teacher might state that 'This is it' and expect the seeker to understand what is meant, the direct-path teacher will begin with a simple observation or statement that everyone can agree with. The direct path does not deny the seeker's viewpoint as often happens in neo-advaita.

Instead, the direct-path method embraces the seeker's initial viewpoint and then gently deconstructs it by combining the seeker's own observations with a stepwise logical progression that reason cannot refute.

156 The direct-path approach as inspired by Sri Atmananda is not specifically mentioned in this book. As of this writing, there are too few teachers who actually use this approach for teaching trends to have emerged.

Neo-advaita

157 'Neo-advaita' is a very recent phenomenon and its principal protagonists were unknown before the mid nineteen-nineties. It is the term used for the style of teaching that purports to express only the final, absolute truth of advaita.

158 Effectively, it states the 'bottom-line' conclusions without having carried out any of the intervening stages. Instead of systematically undermining all of the seeker's pre-existing beliefs, it attempts to supplant them with a radical new belief. This new belief is contrary to everyday (i.e. dualistic) experience and there is no rationale given in justification.

159 Neo-advaita has no methodology, since its teachers explicitly reject the scriptures as a pramANa along with everything else. This aspect is the key to the essence of traditional teaching. Just as the eyes are the means for acquiring knowledge of form and color, the ears the means for acquiring knowledge of sounds and so on, so are the scriptures (together with a teacher who understands the methods) the means for obtaining Self-knowledge.

160 It does not admit of any 'levels' of reality and does not recognize the existence of a seeker, teacher, Self-ignorance, spiritual path etc.

161 Some of the teachers who actually do belong to a traditional sampradAya are also making similar 'absolute' statements about the nature of reality (e.g. recent teachers in the Navnath sampradAya to which Nisargadatta belonged). In doing this (i.e. cutting out all of the intermediate steps in the teaching process), they are effectively distancing themselves from their sampradAya, since they are no longer using the established teaching methodology.

162 Advaita admits of no alternative truths. Consequently, the idea of 'Neo'-advaita is a contradiction. Non-duality by definition is the (only) reality so 'neo-advaita' could not in any way be 'new'. Neither is it "the latest, streamlined version of an outmoded, archaic traditional system" (Ref. 2) But note that it is the (lack of) methodology of neo-advaita that is being criticized, not the name (which some practitioners reject anyway).

163 Despite insisting that there is no one to become enlightened and that this word itself has no meaning, neo-advaitins nevertheless admit that the way that they perceive the world now differs from how they once saw it. And many speak of the (non-)event which triggered this transformation. It is never explained why there is such a reluctance to refer to this (non-)event as 'enlightenment'.

164 If the purpose of teaching is for 'education', i.e. the 'leading out' (Latin 'educere') from ignorance into knowledge, then traditional advaita counts as teaching, neo-advaita doesn't.

165 Neo-advaita is a belief-system without a system – i.e. no structure, no method, no practice; the 'bottom line' without any preceding text.

Reality

166 The confusion between 'reality' and 'appearance' is absolutely fundamental to the problems of the satsang and neo-advaitin

approaches.

167 Traditional teaching begins with whom we think ourselves to be and takes us gradually to an understanding of who we really are.

168 Neo-advaitin teaching begins and ends with attempted, direct statements about the nature of absolute reality and denies empirical reality in the form of everyday appearance and human experience.

169 According to traditional teaching, the 'progress' of the spoken word is from Consciousness (as reflected in the intellect), to visualization of a form that is then framed into language, which is then uttered. This final utterance is far removed from the Consciousness that initiated it. Language is used only as a pointer, back to that Consciousness.

Swami Muni Narayana Prasad: "What a word can do is convey a finite idea, which is only a spark of the infinite and transcendent Consciousness. So if one thinks that he understood the transcendental Truth or brahman, as the meaning of the words he heard from someone, that Truth is only a minute spark of the real infinite Truth, because words do not hold Truth as their meaning." (Ref. 74)

170 Traditional teaching acknowledges that we appear to be separate individuals (persons), living in a world of other people and objects; that we have problems and that we want to be happy. Only after appropriate practices and teaching, do we finally understand the real state of affairs, namely that we are in fact the non-dual brahman (even though we may have been told this from the beginning).

"The Atman, subtlest of the subtle, greatest of the great, is seated in the heart of each living being. He who is free from willing and wishing, with his mind and senses composed, beholds the majesty of the Self and becomes free from sorrow." Katha Upanishad I.2.20

(Ref. 95)

171 Neo-advaitin teaching states that reality is non-dual; that we are already brahman and therefore there is no one to do anything and nothing to realize.

This is effectively nihilism. Here is the definition of that term from the New Oxford English Dictionary: "The rejection of all religious and moral principles, often in the belief that life is meaningless; (in Philosophy) the extreme skepticism maintaining that nothing in the world has a real existence.

172 The inappropriateness of this can be illustrated by a metaphor. Telling students that there is no creation, that there are no objects and no separate person, without having unfolded this gradually and logically, is like telling them that a lump of iron is mainly space. It is true (at a certain level of teaching) that iron is a lattice of iron atoms and that each atom consists of a central nucleus of protons and neutrons surrounded, at a relatively vast distance, by electrons of differing energy. Proportionately, the main 'content' of the atom is space. So, says the student, there will be no adverse effect if I hit you over the head with this lump of space!

173 The point is that advaita is a gauged teaching. The use of unsubstantiated, absolute statements from the latter stages, when talking to the beginning student is more likely to confuse than help. Indeed, traditionally, the Mandukya Upanishad and Gaudapada's commentary are only taught to students who have already studied the other major Upanishads. (It is the Gaudapada kArikA which contains some statements that might be considered analogous to those of the neo-advaitins. The difference is that these are backed by rigorous logical argument.)

In the extreme, this can mean that the seeker who has spent time in western satsangs may actually be worse off than the complete beginner since he or she has an additional level of confusion over and above the usual self-ignorance of the average person.

174 Traditional advaita recognizes three 'levels' of reality: paramArtha - the absolute reality; vyavahAra - the apparent, day-to-day reality; pratibhAsa - the illusory.

175 Another way in which some schools differentiate the orders of reality is satyam (that which is absolutely real), mithyA (that which is neither real nor unreal, but has a 'dependent' reality) and tuchCham (that which is completely unreal).

176 Ultimately, there is only paramArtha but traditional teaching acknowledges the validity of our present experience so that vyavahAra is a necessary fiction to explain this. In keeping with the methodology of adhyAropa apavAda (see 420), it is only naturally spoken of as false when the seeker is able to appreciate that. Also, the apparent world never goes away; after enlightenment, it is simply recognized as mithyA.

[Note that it is not that any teaching is 'held back'. The absolute truth is acknowledged from the outset but the reasoning, which leads to this conclusion, has to be introduced gradually, as the student gains more self-knowledge. The 'final truth' cannot be appreciated by one who is still identified with 'me and mine'.]

177 Most satsang teachers also, at least implicitly, accept the notion of levels. For example, John Wheeler (whose teacher was 'Sailor' Bob Adamson, a direct disciple of Nisargadatta) states that: *"Things matter at the appropriate level of appearance. See the world as a passing appearance and give it the appropriate level of attention."* (Ref. 33)

178 Neo-advaita only recognizes paramArtha.

179 A famous statement, attributed to Shankara sums up the traditional attitude to reality and the apparent world (and, indeed, the whole of advaita): *brahmasatyam jaganmithyA jIvo brahmaiva nA para* - brahman is satyam (truth, reality); jagat (the world) is mithyA; the jIva is nA (not) para (different from) brahman.

180 We mix up real and unreal – adhyAsa. For example, in the sentence 'I am a man', 'I am' is true but 'a man' is mithyA.

181 'A man' and all such attributions are simply names being applied to forms of the non-dual reality.

182 The metaphor frequently used in the scriptures to illustrate this is the ring and gold. Only the gold is real. The ring can be heated up and reformed into something else but the gold exists before, during and after.

183 The traditional definition of 'real' is: that which exists in 'all three periods of time' (trikAlAtIta), past, present and future.

184 The gold is thus real (satyam), the ring is merely mithyA, depending on the gold for its existence. Similarly, we and the world are mithyA, depending on brahman for our existence.

185 Paradoxically, it is knowledge of mithyA that brings about enlightenment, not knowledge of satyam. It is by understanding and rejecting the unreal that we come to know what is real.

186 Since neo-advaitins only acknowledge the real, their teaching is doomed to failure.

Traditional teachers do not attempt to describe reality (instead, they provide 'pointers' to it).

187 A statement by Nathan Gill sums up the neo-advaitin attitude: *"Presently there's simply this – which may include mesmerization with the story of 'me'. If the story of 'me' is what appears to be real presently, then it is reality."* (Ref. 3)

*Undoubtedly, the 'way things are' **is** the way they are (reality is reality) but the way things are **seen** depends on the state of the mind that sees them. The appearance is mithyA, not satyam but the ignorant mind fails to recognize this. We see the form but miss the essence.*

188 Appearance *is* reality but is not initially *known* to be reality. The perceived duality always appears to be real but is ultimately realized to be false.

Appearance

189 We are fighting against a life-time's habit of seeing separateness all around us. Simply being told that reality is non-dual is not going to change anything; the experience remains the same.

It is comparable to being told that everything is made up of protons, electrons and neutrons or that space is curved. This may, indeed, be true but it makes no difference to our immediate experience. Indeed, reality being non-dual and space being curved are probably equally meaningless to most people!

190 The neo-advaitin's refusal to recognize vyavahAra is a fundamental point from which many of the other problems derive. Since there is no vyavahAra, they argue, there is no jIva and hence no seeker, no seeking and nothing to be sought.

This is equivalent to saying that there is only clay and no such thing as a cup – how, then, would we drink our coffee?

191 The fact is that vyavahAra is true *whilst one is in vyavahAra*. This can be regarded as 'objective' reality – there are no objects only in paramArtha. The seeker believes she is the body-mind form. As a result of this ignorance of the truth, there is suffering etc. The world is real from the standpoint of the waker, just as the dream world is real from the standpoint of the dreamer. It is only from the standpoint of turIya (the non-dual reality that is the basis of the waking, dreaming and sleeping states) that the world can be said to be unreal.

"Dream belongs to him who perceives wrongly and sleep to him who knows not Reality. When the false notion of these two comes to an end, the state of turIya is attained." Mandukya Karika I.15 (Ref. 96)

192 The statements of neo-advaitin teachers cannot be made from the standpoint of paramArtha - by definition, since language is part of vyavahAra. For the teacher to speak to a seeker assumes (the appearance of) duality so that it is self-contradictory to use words to deny all of this.

193 It is not possible to describe the *appearance* from the vantage point of *reality* since there is no duality in reality. If we are to speak meaningfully about anything in the appearance, we have to make our stand *in that appearance*. Thus the words can only ever be pointers to the truth.

194 Within vyavahAra, while there is identification, 'I' seem to be suffering. After enlightenment, it is known that I am not that with which I was previously identified. Consequently, although the body and mind may continue to suffer, 'I' do not. So (in the phenomenal realm) there *are* seekers and there can be *enlightenment*.

195 Many of the statements by modern satsang and neo-advaitin teachers confuse paramArtha with vyavahAra and these in turn give rise to considerable misunderstanding on the part of the seeker.

Consider, for example, the claim that practice cannot make the seeker into something that they are not already. But 'the seeker' is at the level of vyavahAra while 'what he or she really is' is at the level of paramArtha. Accordingly, the statement is invalid since it is mixing levels. It is true that the seeker is already the Self but he or she does not realize this. Practice prepares the mind for this realization.

196 Indeed, it often seems to be the case that neo-advaitin teachers intentionally use the absolute statements of paramArtha to quash reasonable objections that are raised at the vyAvahArika level. The seeker is usually insufficiently experienced to be able to spot the contradictions.

197 To the extent that neo-advaitins deny the level of appearance, they also diverge from advaita as taught by Gaudapada. Verse 30 of the Chapter on 'Illusion' in Gaudapada's kArikA on the Mandukya Upanishad states that the true teacher knows that the appearance of duality continues, even though the truth of non-duality is realized. *"This Atman, though non-separate from all these, appears as it were, separate."* (Ref. 61)

Ishvara and mAyA

198 Having admitted the empirical reality of the world, we are obliged to account for its existence.

199 Traditional advaita employs the 'argument from design' logic to argue the existence of a creator who is both the material and efficient cause for creation.

200 The divine principal responsible for the creation is called Ishvara and the power (shakti) that He wields is termed mAyA. This manifests as ignorance or avidyA at the personal level.

201 All of this is regarded as 'effectively' true at the vyAvahArika level. Ishvara and mAyA relate to the macrocosmic or universal whilst jIva and avidyA relate to the microcosmic or individual. All collapses into the non-dual brahman when viewed from the pAramArthika standpoint.

Free Will

202 As noted, from the pAramArthika standpoint there is no separate individual person, there is only brahman. brahman is not a doer; brahman does not act. It follows therefore that, for brahman there is no free will and no predestination; there are no actions and no events because there is no time, space or causality.

203 However, the seeker starts with the belief that the world-appearance is real, that he is a doer and does have free will. Traditional advaita teaches that we are where and how we are as a result of past, 'freely' chosen actions (karma). At each moment, our scope for action is partly pre-determined (according to the 'fruit' of past actions) and partly free. The motive behind the action may again generate new saMskAra. This is a complex (and emotive!) topic – for a detailed discussion, see Ref. 2).

[Whenever an action is performed with the desire for a specific result (whether for oneself or another), saMskAra-s are created for that person. These accumulate and determine the situations with which we will be presented in the future and will influence the scope of our actions.]

204 This is an important point in the comparison of traditional and neo-advaitin presentations. Traditionally, we do have limited choice and

we do act. And, 'as we act, so do we reap' – the motivation for action or attachment to the results of action entrenches us deeper in the mire of saMsAra. In contrast, the neo-advaitin claims that we do not act and have no choice; this clearly implies that what we do makes no difference. This is a rash, uninformed and potentially damaging doctrine.

205 It makes more sense to regard yourself as a separate person with free will for the time being, since this is how it feels. The results of your actions then have consequences (the so-called law of karma) and so on. In the end, it will be discovered that the bottom-line statements of the neo-advaitins are true (in the sense that who-we-really are – brahman – has no free will) but, to begin with, they are of no help at all. It is a well-established fact that the gaining of self-knowledge is a step-wise affair. It is simply not possible to reach the top of the stairs without treading on any of the intervening steps.

And the enlightened man still chooses whether to have tea or coffee! (Though he brings about no more saMskAra-s or binding likes, dislikes, attachments or aversions in the process.)

Enlightenment

206 Many seekers visit satsangs, ostensibly to become enlightened, without having any prior understanding of non-duality or even the meaning of 'enlightenment'.

207 Since the premise of the book is that satang teaching alone does not bring about enlightenment, it is most important that the reader is clear what this term means.

208 The formal, traditional explanation of the meaning of enlightenment or mokSha was given in the key definitions section at the beginning of the book. The present section has two parts (in addition to this introduction). The first presents some of the mistaken views and the following lists those aspects that are correct (according to traditional advaita).

209 Those seekers who have been exposed to advaita philosophy to any significant degree should have a good idea what is meant by enlightenment, even if they are not able to formulate a clear definition themselves. But those who are new to 'seeking' or who have only previously encountered 'New Age' concepts probably have varied and mistaken ideas. In recent years, the popularization of the topic has inevitably devalued its true meaning and those who have only attended neo-advaita satsangs may have an entirely wrong perception.

210 Many seekers are therefore in the difficult situation of aiming for a goal without really appreciating the nature of that goal (imagine a soccer match in which the player intentionally kicks the ball at the corner flag in order to score). If their understanding is wide of the mark, it could present a serious obstacle.

211 Seeking enlightenment is a lifetime commitment, not a casual

pastime, and is incompatible with the aspirations of most people, especially those in the materialistic West. Only those who are convinced that happiness will not be found in possessions or achievements and who are looking for meaning and purpose to their lives are likely to be interested.

212 Finally, it should be noted that the whole of this section relates to enlightenment itself – j~nAna – and not to the 'secondary' benefits (jIvanmukti) that may or may not accrue (see 341).

What Enlightenment is not

213 Enlightenment has nothing to do with 'merging with the Self' or 'becoming one with God'. In reality, we are already the Self so that these expressions could have no meaning. Nor is it a 'feeling of unity'.

When a pot is broken, the 'pot space' does not merge with the 'total space'; the 'total space' is entirely unaffected by the presence of the container and remains the same before, during and after the temporary appearance of the pot.

214 It is not about 'returning to God' in any sense. Some think that the Self has somehow 'become' all of the jIva-s and that this is the meaning of saMsAra. They presume that now the jIva in turn has to 'become' the Self or paramAtman and that this constitutes enlightenment. But the paramAtman can never become anything since it is all pervasive and not subject to change.

Gaudapada states in his commentary on the Mandukya Upanishad (IV.7): "Of that being which is ever unborn, birth is predicated by some; but it is impossible that the unborn and the immortal could ever partake of the mortal." (Ref. 92)

215 The 'truth' about enlightenment is not 'higher' (or 'lower'), does

not 'come from within' or 'from the heart', nor is it 'channeled' from some other-worldly being or god. All these are typical but mistaken, mystical ideas about enlightenment.

216 Enlightenment is not about 'experiencing the Self' - otherwise everyone would be enlightened. It is not about experience at all, it is about self-knowledge - the direct knowledge that you are already that which you seek. (See 25 - 97.)

217 Nor is enlightenment itself an experience - experiences come and go. Enlightenment is not temporary - once it happens, that is it. Consequently, if you had an experience and wonder whether you are now enlightened, you can be sure that you are not. Also, there is no need for a seeker to try to recapture a 'good' experience, thinking that it was somehow closer to enlightenment than the usual 'bad' experiences. (See 102 to 104)

218 But this is not to say that experiences whilst 'on the path' are not useful in the sense of providing encouragement to continue.

219 Enlightenment is not a 'state' – these also come and go.

220 Nor can you have 'periods' of enlightenment or varying depths or degrees – you are either enlightened or not.

221 It is pedantically true that there is no such thing as 'gradual enlightenment'. As noted in 94, however, there is another potential misunderstanding of terms here. It is true that you cannot be 'partly' enlightened – you either are or you are not – but the removal of self-ignorance can certainly be gradual.

222 There is much confusion about 'who' it is that gains enlightenment. Clearly the non-dual Self, brahman, cannot become enlightened and yet the ultimate truth is that there is no separate entity, no satyam

'ego' or 'person'.

Jean Klein (who was essentially a direct-path teacher) said: "Liberation does not concern the person, for liberation is freedom from the person." (Ref. 48) Tony Parsons (who is a neo-advaitin teacher) says: "There is no such thing as an 'enlightened person'. No person has ever been 'enlightened'." (Ref. 47) Jean Klein is correct to the extent that he uses the word 'liberation'; Tony Parsons is wrong since he uses the word 'enlightened'. N.B. Remember the definition of person given in 105 to 109. It is the jIva who gains enlightenment, and it takes place in the mind as is explained in 99.

223   Enlightenment is not about becoming 'free' - the Self is already free; it is about realizing this fact in the mind.

224   The search for enlightenment begins with ahaMkAra as the key element. It is the identified mind that wants to become enlightened. In the end, the mind recognizes that who I *really* am is not the mind; I am brahman, the non-dual reality. The mind is merely an instrument.

225   The confusion arises again from mixing up empirical and absolute reality (vyavahAra and paramArtha). The absolute truth is that there are no things or persons but the world, objects and people still appear as forms, which are thought to be separate and real by the ignorant mind.

226   Those teachers (principally neo-advaitin ones) who claim that there is no such thing as enlightenment are trying, as always, to speak from the absolute reality standpoint. But this should be made very clear. If they say that, for example, 'here and now, for the seeker, there is no enlightenment', then they are wrong and are deluding themselves, as well as the seeker.

227 Enlightenment is not about fulfilling your ambitions, or about getting all of the things that you always wanted but which life was unable to provide (but note 341). Enlightenment is the realization that all ambitions and motivations no longer matter, although they may still arise after enlightenment as a result of prArabdha karma (the fruit of past actions).

228 It is not about providing meaning and purpose in your life - there can be none from the standpoint of absolute reality. Subsequent to enlightenment, needless to say, life takes on a new significance.

229 Enlightenment is not about becoming 'special' so that everyone holds you in high regard.

230 It is not about being permanently blissful or even just 'feeling good' all the time. Indeed, there will still be 'pain'; what disappears is 'suffering', in the sense of a 'me' who owns the pain.

231 But enlightenment does bring freedom from suffering.

It is belief in a separate I, in which ahaMkAra is identified with a body and mind (i.e. subject to the positive and negative events that take place in duality) that is the cause of suffering.

232 It is not about making you 'better' in any sense; not about self-help or self-improvement. You are already perfect and complete. (Although the mind is 'improved' as a result of j~nAna phalam – see 341.)

233 But, although it is true that we are 'already the Self', and that the non-dual reality is 'already the case' we do not presently realize this. Accordingly it makes no sense to say, as some neo-advaitin teachers do, that 'This' is enlightenment.

234 It is not having a permanently empty mind. Thoughts (and even desires) will still arise (see 250).

235 It is not about being more open and responsive to others – this may indeed happen but enlightenment is the recognition that there are no 'others'. (It is also acceptance of the *appearance* of duality and separate persons.) Neither is it about ceasing to be responsive because this is known. Empathy and open-heartedness follow naturally because it is known that everything is brahman, my Self.

236 It has nothing to do with 'energy', nor is it a 'force'; it is not something 'external' that enters the person. It is not a light in any literal sense, nor does it make you less heavy in anything other than a metaphorical sense.

Physical manifestations of light, whether 'flashes' or 'blinding' do not signal enlightenment but are a sign that one may need to visit the doctor.

237 Similarly, 'inner voices' or 'messages from the heart' invariably arise from the mind and, irrespective of spiritual content, usually relate to the ego.

238 Enlightenment is not 'timeless'. On the contrary, it is an event in time, in vyavahAra.

239 It is not the next evolutionary step in mankind's development. Nor does it have anything to do with the individual soul evolving into a superior state.

240 There is no 'higher Self' that we have to 'reach' – there is only *the* Self.

241 It is not about 'self-transcendence' (whatever that might be). There

is no such thing as 'transcendental living.' (But the practical life of the realized man will be very different from that of the typical materialist since what is transcended is the notion that 'I am this body' - dehAtma buddhi.)

242   It is not an 'expansion of consciousness'; it is not 'within' us (or without). Consciousness is already everywhere and always.

243   There are no 'levels' or 'realms' of consciousness to 'pass through' on the road to enlightenment. As Ramesh Balsekar famously puts it (quoting from his teacher, Nisargadatta Maharaj): *"Consciousness is all there is."*

244   Enlightenment is not about altered states of awareness. Enlightenment is not a state and Consciousness is the reality of all apparent states, in the same way that gold is the reality of rings, bangles and chains.

245   It has nothing to do with 'rising' (or falling) or 'going deeper'.

246   Enlightenment does not grant immortality. It has nothing to do with the body. The body-mind *will* die regardless. Who you really are is already immortal.

"It was not born; It will never die: nor once having been, can It ever cease to be: Unborn, Eternal, Ever-enduring, yet Most Ancient, the Spirit dies not when the body is dead." Bhagavad Gita II.20 (Ref. 97)

247   Nor does it mean that you will cease to exist. Who you really are is ever existent. Who you think you are, such as the body/mind, is always changing and, when investigated, cannot be found to exist in the ultimate sense of the word.

This body and mind continues as before, eating, sleeping and dreaming. Indeed, outwardly, there may be little to indicate that anything is any different.

248 It is not something to be achieved in order that we can help mankind. In fact it does not have anything to do with humanity (except that only man has a mind capable of becoming enlightened).

249 It is not about escaping from life and becoming a hermit, nor about removing oneself from a world of desired objects. It has nothing to do with freeing oneself from the world in an empirical sense. It has to do with freeing the mind from believing that the world affects who you really are.

250 Enlightenment does not mean an end to desire; desires may still arise and be acted upon or not; they then disappear and are forgotten. The ultimate purpose of desire is the wish to return to the Self. They therefore no longer serve any useful function once the Self has been realized. Thus, we become free from dependence upon the satisfaction of our desires.

Traditional Vedanta would say that desires may still continue to arise in the mind of the j~nAnI as a result of that person's prArabdha karma but they can be expected to diminish in both frequency and intensity. The j~nAnI knows that the fulfilment of any desire is not the actual cause of happiness, but desires may keep on arising in the mind and keep on being fulfilled in the creation, as one's karma dictates. The key difference is that the belief that "I need that (person, thing or situation) in order to be happy," is no longer present, since the mind knows that the locus of happiness is my Self. Accordingly, selfish desires will naturally tend to fall away.

251 Enlightenment is not about 'being in the present', specifically, although longing for the past or worrying about the future will no

longer be a concern post-enlightenment.

It will not be a concern because I now know that, whatever the outcome, it will not affect who-I-really-am. (Everything happens according to cause-effect law within the apparent creation.)

252 Becoming enlightened does not mean that we will become 'all-knowing' or endowed with special psychic powers, able to see into the future or read people's minds; we will not be all-powerful, able to perform super-human tasks or hold dominion over others.

It has been claimed by some teachers that so-called siddhi-s (super-natural powers) may arise incidentally for some seekers but any attachment to these will only postpone enlightenment. But, whether or not they actually exist (within vyavahAra), they form no part of traditional advaita.

253 Feelings of ecstasy, visions of God, yogic flying, astral projections and other *"pastimes and drugs, and features of the press"* (Ref. 8) have nothing to do with enlightenment. Nor do bright lights, visions, hallucinations or premonitory dreams.

254 Going without sleep or food, controlling the breathing, slowing the heartbeat or any other bodily or mental modification will not bring about enlightenment.

255 Drugs may bring about mystical experiences but they will never bring enlightenment.

256 Enlightenment is not about expanding the mind.

257 Nor is enlightenment about a still or silent mind; it is about a mind that directly knows the nature of the Self.

258 It has nothing to do with kuNDalinI yoga or chakra-s.

259 Becoming enlightened does not mean that the world ceases to exist.

The advaita theory of ajAtivAda means that there has never been any creation, but the world as an appearance of name and form continues as before; it is simply now known to be not other than our Self. This is widely misunderstood.

260 Enlightenment cannot be transmitted by a teacher (e.g. by 'laying-on' of hands etc.)

Philip Mistlberger: "It can be confirmed or recognized by another, but it always arises from within as a direct, tacit realization of who and what we actually are." (Ref. 24)

What Enlightenment is

261 So, what is enlightenment? There are many descriptions and definitions and those in New-Age type books should generally be completely ignored. Epithets with capitalized letters or containing familiar words with unfamiliar endings (usually '-ness') should generally be avoided.

262 In reality, there is only brahman (the non-dual, beginningless, endless, Absolute existence) and it is obviously not meaningful to speak of brahman becoming enlightened - brahman IS without any limit.

263 At the level of the apparent world however, there appear to be jIva-s as a result of Atman seemingly being limited by self-ignorance. Why this should be the case is not a question that can meaningfully be addressed. So, as already noted, there is effectively a person who becomes enlightened when that self-ignorance is removed in the mind (see 98 - 99 and 105 - 109).

264 In truth, there is only the non-dual reality - call this the Atman. Nevertheless, there is usually a firm belief that 'I am a separate person'. The 'entity which has this thought' is called the jIva in traditional advaita. You, the jIva, are clearly not enlightened while the Atman is already free. Enlightenment occurs when you, the jIva, realize that you are in fact the Atman (and simultaneously cease to believe that you are a jIva).

*In the metaphor, the snake does not have to **become** the rope – there never was a snake. What is needed is knowledge of this.*

265 The metaphor of wave and ocean is often wrongly understood in this context. Who-I-think-I-am is equated to the wave, while the reality is equated to the ocean. This can give the misleading impression that I am a *part* of the ocean. This is a misinterpretation. In fact, the point of the illustration is that there is only water. The form of the wave is certainly a part of the form of the ocean. This equates to saying that the jIva is a part of Ishvara. But both ocean and wave are the same water – I am not a *part* of brahman; I *am* brahman.

266 From the point of view of the 'person' in the apparent world, enlightenment is an event in time. But, subsequent to enlightenment, it is known that there never was a person; that I was already free. Both the world and the person are only appearances of name and form and time is only a concept.

N.B. From the point of view of an unenlightened observer in the world, the enlightened 'person' (called a j~nAnI), still continues to exist and go about his or her usual business. And the j~nAnI continues to act and utilize concepts of time, space and causality just as before. The difference is that it is now known that the world is mithyA and all is, in reality, brahman.)

267 It is not that I will become free at some time in the future. If that were the case, freedom would be finite and therefore not eternal (and could come to an end also). In fact I am eternally free. What occurs in time is simply the recognition of this fact. This is best referred to as 'enlightenment', since the term 'liberation' implies that I am being freed. (See the 'Key definition' at the beginning of the book.)

268 One metaphor for the process might be the 'Magic Eye' paintings, which appear at first sight to be simply a random pattern of colored dots. This appearance may be sustained for a very long time until, suddenly, without consciously realizing what change has occurred, a three-dimensional image suddenly manifests on the page.

269 In fact, the situation is much worse than this because:
a. We have to reject the 'evidence' of our senses and the supposed reality of separate objects and persons.
b. We must understand that materialism and science, valuable though they may be, have little to say about non-physical reality.
c. We need to see through our indoctrination by thousands of years of Western culture with its accepted 'truths' of mind, individuality, material values and so on.
d. We are conditioned forever to seek answers objectively. The idea that the subject who is observing these objects cannot itself be investigated objectively is one which is alien to us.

270 Enlightenment is about ceasing to identify with the notion of being a person (or any object that exists in time or space). It is to see through the illusion that we are separate - from anything or anyone; there are no 'others' – 'we' are all one.

271 It is about the direct recognition that 'I am brahman' and always have been (and so is 'everything else').

272 This is why the question of 'being enlightened or not' is a tricky one to answer, because it really depends upon the understanding of the one who is asking. Since it is almost certainly the case that the question is being asked from the vantage point of a 'person', it is probably best to answer from the same point of view. Thus, to answer "yes, I am an enlightened person" should be perfectly acceptable (and can be pedantically true) within vyavahAra.

The following is how Philip Kapleau Roshi replied to the question (Ref. 54, quoted in Ref. 53): "If I say 'yes, I am enlightened,' those of you who know will walk out in disgust. If I say, 'No, I am not enlightened,' those of you who misunderstand will walk out disappointed."

273 It is about the 'elusive obvious' as one (neo-advaitin) teacher (Roger Linden) has called it, suddenly seeing what was always the case; self-evident once seen, yet revelatory at the time of seeing. He uses the example of the drawings which can be seen in different ways (e.g. either as a vase or as two faces). Initially it may be extremely difficult to see one of the representations but, suddenly, it 'clicks' and then you cannot help but see it.

274 Enlightenment is freedom from self-ignorance and self-delusion (avidyA) - this is effectively the definition given by Gaudapada in his exposition (kArikA) on the Mandukya Upanishad.

275 Enlightenment means freedom from the notion that I need to become enlightened.

276 It is the end of 'becoming', because the seeker no longer takes herself to be that which is subject to becoming or change, including being born or dying.

277 It means no longer looking towards external things or people in

order to find fulfillment or happiness. It is complete freedom from dependence on anything or anyone.

As Swami Dayananda puts it, enlightenment is the end we all want, namely the end of all wants. (Ref. 52)

278 It is the final understanding that one is already whole and complete - pUrNam - and without limit - anantam.

279 But it is not a superficial understanding; it is a deep and unshakeable certainty that goes beyond mere belief. Any concept that might cast doubts has been eradicated and there is no longer any possibility that a new doubt might arise.

280 Enlightenment is always to know that reality is non-dual despite the seeming duality of the world.

281 It is not denial of the world but acceptance of its apparent duality and knowledge that it *is* only apparent.

282 Having become enlightened, I recognize that the world of objects is mithyA and thereby remove its power to cause suffering and prolong saMsAra.

283 Enlightenment may be achieved as a result of following various practices (sAdhanA) such as meditation, gaining knowledge through study of the scriptures, becoming the disciple of a guru and so on. (See 355 for the traditional method of shravaNa etc.)

The Atmabodha (one of the texts attributed to Shankara) compares the fact that brahman 'pervades' everything to the way that butter 'exists' in milk. In order to 'realize' the butter, the milk must undergo the 'sAdhanA' of extraction - boiling, cooling, adding curd and so on. Similarly, the sAdhanA of the seeker brings about increasingly clearly, the direct knowledge that 'I am already brahman'. (Ref. 14)

284 It is because enlightenment is effectively an 'event' in the mind that the mind must be prepared so that the event is able to take place. The clearing of obstacles to realization, and the increasing clarity of the subject matter in the mind of the student (direct understanding), are aided through certain practices. These practices enable the mind to gain gradual but direct understanding, as well as the final 'Self-knowledge' (akhaNDAkAra) vRRitti.

285 The reason for different 'paths', as Philip Mistlberger points out (Ref. 24) is that paths are for deconstructing the ego, and its variations are legion. The Self is already the Self and doesn't need any path to get to where it already is.

286 Neo-advaitins repeatedly tell us that 'I' cannot become enlightened since 'I' do not exist. But there is very good reason why 'I' am unable to accept this. The simple fact is that I know that I *do* exist – it is the single thing about which there is no possible doubt. The problem is that the mind is mistakenly identifying who I really am with the body and mind – the 'person' – this is the ignorance that needs to be corrected. When this occurs, it is not 'I' who becomes enlightened, since I am already brahman; it is the mind (buddhi) that realizes this truth. Enlightenment is the dissociation of the truth of 'I' from the prior identification with mind and body.

Shankara says: "It is to the intellect and not to the Self which is immutable that the knowledge 'I am brahman' belongs." (Ref. 81) [In Sanskrit, buddhi is that function of the mind responsible for discrimination and judgment; frequently translated as 'intellect'.]

287 It is notable that, despite claiming that enlightenment is not something to be attained, these same teachers often write about their own 'enlightenment experience.'

If you doubt that enlightenment is of the mind, ask yourself whether an 'enlightened man' would remain enlightened if his brain, memory and reasoning functions were severed. 'He' would still be the non-dual reality of course, as he always was, before and after enlightenment, but that body-mind form would no longer know this fact.

288   The traditional view is that there is an individual seeker (a jIva), who is motivated to seek the truth.

289   The extreme neo-advaitin position is that this is untrue. Most other satsang teachers appear to hold intermediate positions. The differences will be considered under four separate, section headings:
a. (The claim that there is) No Doer - The idea that there is no 'doer' to begin with and therefore 'no seeker.'
b. (The claim that there is) Nothing to Do - The idea that there is nothing that needs to be done - we are already 'That'; already enlightened etc. There is therefore 'nothing to be sought.'
c. (The claim that there is) No Path - The idea that, irrespective of the above, nothing could be done to bring about enlightenment anyway; all doing is for the ego and only results in something for 'me'. There cannot, therefore, be any 'spiritual path' to enlightenment.
d. (The claim that there is) No Practice - The idea that, consequently, no 'practices' can ever help us either to prepare for a path or to follow one.

(The claim that there is) No Doer

290 It is fundamental to the final teaching of all non-dual philosophies that there are no separate entities.

291 Consequently, in reality (paramArtha), there is no one who 'does' anything.

The apparent 'doing' is simply the changing names and forms of the (apparently) manifest creation in accordance with causality. The Bhagavad Gita tells us that we are the awareness in which action takes place but we ourselves do not act (IV.18); we believe ourselves to be a doer but action is performed by the guNa-s (III.27). [Nature is 'made up of' three guNa-s or 'ingredients' in sAMkhya philosophy – see glossary.]

292 However, although in reality there is no doer, at the relative level (vyavahAra) I appear to be a doer through the medium of the body-mind upAdhi. At this level, events take place and there are individuals with free will who perform actions which have conse-quences. [upAdhi is often translated as 'limiting adjunct'. It literally means something that is put in place of another thing; a substitute, phantom or disguise. Effectively, it refers to one of the 'identifica-tions' made by ahaMkAra that prevents us from realizing the Self.]

293 The neo-advaitin view *only* acknowledges the absolute, ultimate, pAramArthika viewpoint, insisting that there is no person; only a 'story' about a person. This story may include following a spiritual path and becoming enlightened or not – it makes no difference to anything.

Needless to say, this position is not very helpful as far as the seeker is concerned. She still feels that she very much exists and wants to escape from her suffering etc. Furthermore, this is a very misleading statement for the seeker. The truth of the situation is that 'I am' or 'I exist' is the one thing about which I can be absolutely certain. I may negate everything else but I could never negate this, since 'I' would have to exist in order to do the negating. Therefore, in order to understand such a statement, the seeker must be able to differentiate between 'I' and 'me, the person'. The neo-advaitins never provide the teaching that would enable the seeker to do this, since such a distinction can only be made in the context of vyavahAra.

294 Since there is no one, argues the neo-advaitin, there cannot be such a process as 'identification' to bring about the false notion of separation.

This is effectively a statement about the ontological status of self-ignorance. The unarguable fact of the matter is that there is self-ignorance in vyavahAra. It is, however, not possible to say how or when this arose – it is said to be anirvachanIya, meaning that it is inexplicable. This may be seen in the rope-snake metaphor. If you ask when the rope-ignorance began and the snake appeared, you will find that the question is unanswerable. If you claim that it began in the moment that you looked at the rope, this would have to mean that before that moment there was knowledge of the rope. This would make no sense. We have to say that the ignorance is begin-ningless – anAdi.

295 To the extent that enlightenment means anything at all, say the neo-advaitins, we are already enlightened.

*This mistake was pointed out in the definition at the beginning of the book – the Self is already free but the mind does not know this, i.e. as long as we believe that we are the mind, 'we' are **not** enlightened. The knowledge that there is no need to seek is lacking. The 'liber-ation' is from the notion that we were ever bound.*

296 The claim that there is no doer and no one who can choose to do anything is frequently used by neo-advaitins to conclude that no spiritual path can be chosen or could be effective in bringing about enlightenment.

But this is to confuse levels of reality as explained in 166 to 197. The jIva, who is the one who needs the path, is at the relative level of the world. It is only brahman who, in reality, is not a doer that does not need any path.

297 But the statement is a fallacy in any case. We may not accept the traditional view that free will is available at the empirical level of existence or that grace is 'earned' as a result of past action. Even so, a path can still be *effectively* chosen as a result of the combination of the nature of the seeker and the (chance) happening of external events, e.g. reading a particular book, hearing about an Internet Egroup and looking to see what is being discussed there etc.

298 Such activities could be considered to be automatic, carried out without there being 'anyone' or any free will and yet lead inexorably to a wearing away of the self-ignorance.

299 Conversely, the mere stating of the absolute truth will have no effect. Even if they can accept it intellectually, seekers still believe deep down that they are a separate body-mind.

300 The simple truth is that the techniques of traditional advaita are effective in removing the delusion that 'I am a separate individual'. If 'I', believing myself to be a person, follow such a path, the outcome is the loss of this delusion, not the augmentation of it.

*Again, it must be emphasized that, at the relative level, I **do** exist and **do** act. There is a mind that suffers and seeks to remove this suffering. This is the 'seeker'.*

301 Traditional teaching specifically aims to enable us to 'see through' the ahaMkAra. The ego-sense is resolved as a result of understanding, not via edict or choice. You cannot choose to have the akhaNDAkAra vRRitti or give it to someone - it arises when the mind is ready. One does have the limited ability to choose actions which will influence the quality of the mind which will then be more conducive for the occurrence of akhaNDAkAra vRRitti.

302 Conversely, not doing anything will not achieve anything – no cause, no effect – and the seeker remains trapped at her current level of ignorance, with the concomitant frustration and suffering.

303 The logical implication of the 'no cause and effect' position is that anything can happen any time. If this were the case, there could never be any point to any action, since the result would be totally unpredictable.

304 The fact is (and this is in accord with everyone's own experience) that things in this world happen strictly according to natural law, one of which is that effects have causes. Consequently, false notions are dispelled through the logical teaching methodologies which Vedanta employs, and these lead the student's mind to the direct seeing of what is actually true.

305 Even neo-advaitins have to concede that things happen, even if they claim that there isn't actually an entity present that brings them about.

Thus, for example, even if one denies the existence of free will, exercise keeps the body fit and healthy; over-eating tends to make it fat and unhealthy. This is the operation of the simple law of cause and effect. It makes no difference whether or not there is actually someone 'choosing' or 'doing' anything.

306 Traditional advaita uses the theory of karma to explain why it is that outcomes are sometimes unexpected – we are reaping the fruit of past actions; i.e. a clear cause and effect mechanism even when none can be clearly discerned.

307 The claim that there is no seeker or teacher is effectively negated as soon as the neo-advaitin teacher holds satsang. He gives lie to the proclaimed beliefs as soon as he speaks, for this assumes another to whom the words are addressed. It also seems that the neo-teacher is admitting something might change in the seekers as a result of 'teaching' them. Otherwise, what would be the point of 'teaching'?

308 Since they deny the existence of a seeker or enlightenment, neo-advaitins obviously also deny the value of mumukShutva (the intense longing for enlightenment, to the exclusion of all other desires.) But this is one of the key requirements of the seeker according to Shankara.

mumukShutva is a desire to satisfy the highest need of man – to know himself. In just the same way that we desire food when hungry and water when thirsty, when all of those basic desires are satisfied to some degree, we may discover the desire to understand the nature of ourselves and the universe. Traditionally, the scriptures exist to satisfy this need. Once this final desire is realized, one is free from all desires and thereby 'liberated'.

309 Despite all these negations, neo-advaitins often imply that the 'seeing-through of the story' brings with it a sense of freedom, light, love, etc. The inference is that there is a state 'prior' to this event, when there is the sense of being an individual and a state 'after' it, when there is no longer any sense of separation. It does seem that this event in time could usefully be called 'enlightenment', for want of a better word.

310 Speaking of enlightenment as 'the story is seen through' might appear to make some sort of sense but the use of the passive form begs the question of who is doing the seeing. The usual way out of this is to say "It is seen by no one that...", which of course makes no sense at all. To perceive requires a perceiver and a perceived and this is firmly in the realm of appearance (vyavahAra). Who we really are is That which illumines the body/mind and all cognitive perception.

311 This concern with the paradox of there not actually being a 'person' to become enlightened need not be a problem. The point is that, if advaita is taught in a logical and graduated way, the explanation comes about quite naturally. (See 105 - 109 for clarification of the term 'person'.)

(The claim that there is) Nothing to Do

312   Given the basic premise of a non-dual reality, we must already be That (brahman).

313   Logically, therefore, it would seem at first sight that it cannot make any sense that something needs to be done to bring this about. Tony Parsons asks: *"But who is it that is going to choose to make the effort? There is no separate individual volition. How can an illusion dispel itself?"* (Ref. 37)

314   But this is the usual confusion of reality and appearance. In the empirical world, there are people who act. Effort to gain direct self-knowledge may eventually bring about realization. No effort will at best maintain the status quo.

315   The confusion arises because of the failure to differentiate between being and knowing. We cannot do anything to *be* That which we already are but we can do something to remove our ignorance of the fact – namely seek self-knowledge.

Shankara says (commentary on Bhagavad Gita XVIII 50): "Therefore it is not for the knowledge (of brahman or the Self) that any effort is needed; it is needed only to prevent us from regarding the not-Self as the Self." (Ref. 87)

316   Traditional teachers recognize this and provide authentic teaching methods, which remove the erroneous views by pointing out what is actually true in such a way that the seeker sees this, too.

317   Neo-advaitin teachers explain the world-appearance as 'mesmerization' (a term coined by Nathan Gill, as noted earlier).

318   This is counter-productive, since it turns the seeker away from any

self-enquiry that might resolve the conflict.

319 The problem could be viewed as the seeker asking questions from the standpoint of vyavahAra (the apparent world of everyday experience) and the neo-teacher responding from a pAramArthika (absolute reality) viewpoint without actually offering the questioner any help at the level of his misunderstanding.

At best this is likely to lead to 'crossed wires' and a lack of understanding on the part of the seeker; at worst to frustration or depression and an abandoning of seeking altogether. What he or she fundamentally wants to know is "what should I do (at the level of vyavahAra) in order to realize the truth". A response of 'there is no seeker and nothing to be sought; there is no you who can do anything' is certainly true from a pAramArthika standpoint – but it doesn't answer the question!

320 The 'nothing to do' attitude is an effective dismissal of karma yoga as a sAdhanA.

321 Equally, neo-advaitins do not recognize bhakti yoga – they regard devotion to a god as duality and therefore illusory.

All practice, all seeking, seeker and sought are at the level of vyavahAra, where all of this is taking place. So both karma and bhakti yoga are valid practices for preparing the mind to receive Self-knowledge (j~nAna yoga).

322 The implication that 'nothing *needs* to happen' (in order to become enlightened) is also erroneous. What needs to happen is akhaNDAkAra vRRitti in the mind (see 99) Then this particular instantiation of mind and Consciousness (i.e. 'person') becomes 'enlightened' – and knowingly ceases to be identified with any upAdhi.

323 The resolution of the problem is as follows: advaita is vastu-tantra (governed by reality), not kartRRi-tantra (the result of doership), so that it is true that I cannot 'do' anything to bring about self-knowledge. I.e. Non-duality is already the case and nothing I do could ever change that fact. But the knowledge that this is so is only likely to arise in the presence of a qualified teacher unfolding the scriptures, when the seeker's mind is 'ready'. This is the purpose of practice and 'paths' – to prepare the mind and provide pointers to enable self-knowledge to take place spontaneously. As the teaching reveals the truth, self-knowledge automatically arises – I do not have to do anything.

Swami Dayananda uses the metaphor of light and darkness for Self-knowledge and Self-ignorance. He says: "Darkness cannot be removed by any action, but only by light. Similarly, ignorance cannot be removed by any action, because action is not opposed to ignorance; action is a product of ignorance... You cannot say darkness doesn't exist. Until light comes, it exists. A thing that is non-existent cannot create problems, only a thing that exists can create problems. Ignorance of the self is something that exists; it creates problems, it creates error, and it creates a sense of limitation." (Ref. 52)

324 If nothing is done, nothing will happen! The 'person' will continue in his or her life of suffering. Of course this is irrelevant at the level of reality - after all 'I am brahman' – but to the ignorant jIva it makes all the difference. Simply hearing the message repeated is not on its own sufficient, as many satsang seekers will testify. If the basic understanding is not present, the message will simply be unintelligible.

"The disciple said: Not even the word meaning do I fully grasp clearly; how can I then comprehend the significance of the sentence, 'I am Brahman'?" vAkya vRRitti v.9 (Ref. 89)

325 The metaphor of the dream is often used in traditional advaita to clarify the problems that we seem to have in the waking state. If we find that we are ill in a dream, the only remedy is to visit the dream doctor. It makes no difference that 'in reality' there is nothing wrong with us – this is only discovered when we eventually wake up. The same is true regarding our seemingly unenlightened condition in the waking state. The only remedy is to go to a teacher who can address our apparent problems.

326 Being repeatedly told that there is nothing to do, that 'this is it', may be comforting to the Western mindset but it carries with it the very great danger of increasing frustration and helplessness. This might indeed be the intention of neo-advaita, namely to take away the props that hold up the ignorant position of the ego, but if it fails to do so (as, I suggest it fails in the vast majority of cases) it leaves the seeker in a very vulnerable and directionless situation. Furthermore, the teacher is unable to help since she has said all that she can say.

327 Knowing that you exist is not the same as knowing that you are brahman. After all, we have the 'experience' of non-duality every day (in deep sleep) but most people still live out their lives in the mistaken belief that reality is dual and that happiness depends upon getting a good job/house/spouse or whatever. This is **not** it!
We had the experience but missed the meaning,
And approach to the meaning restores the experience
In a different form, beyond any meaning
We can assign to happiness. T.S. Eliot (Ref. 8)

328 Simply making the statement 'you are That' (tat tvam asi) will have no effect on the beginning seeker. It is necessary to go step by step, using progressive logic, until the end statement is arrived at. Only the traditional approach, using the proven methodology, will bring clarity and true understanding. Simply presenting the final statement will leave all of the confusion beneath untreated.

A metaphor might be painting over a diseased piece of wood without first treating the infection. It might appear at first sight that the decoration is sound but, in time, the mold will come through and it will be as if the wood had never been painted.

329 There is also the danger that you may come to believe that you are enlightened yet remain essentially in ignorance.

330 Traditional advaita seeks to clarify all this confusion, not perpetuate it. Neo-advaita just ignores it (and may even make the situation worse).

331 The pace of modern Western society is simply not conducive to spiritual seeking or practice. Nowadays, people expect quick results and are unwilling to accept that the gaining of this knowledge is likely to take a long time and require effort, patience and discipline. It is hardly surprising that any method that tells the seeker that what they seek is already the case is likely to prove popular.

But as already pointed out, this statement is false. The seeker is already free but does not know this. What he wants is to gain the self-knowledge, not the freedom.

332 Finally, those who have been attending satsangs for some time may well believe that they already know most of it already and will be most reluctant to accept that they may need to drop all of it and start again. They may be even more reluctant to admit this to their peers!

(The claim that there is) No Path

333 Since, according to the neo-advaitin, there is no seeker, nothing to be sought, no doer and nothing to be done in order to be what we already are, it also follows that there can be no path.

334 This apparent self-consistency of neo-advaitin teaching is one of its principal attractions and what make it so difficult to argue against. The key, as is so often the case, is in confusing real and apparent. The truth of the Self is at the level of non-dual reality while seeker and teacher are at the level of empirical reality, where seeking does effectively take place. This self-knowledge can only be revealed in the mind of the seeker.

335 Spiritual seeking of the traditional kind creates and strengthens a 'spiritual ego', according to the neo-advaitin. Since 'enlightenment' equates to loss of ego, seeking must therefore be counterproductive.

It is not necessarily the case that any 'spiritual ego' is created, especially for those who are, by nature, sincere and humble and are only seeking self-knowledge. A 'spiritual ego' may equally be created for those neo-advaitin 'non-seekers' who hold such views and think themselves superior!

336 The ego of seeking is not an obstacle (in fact, it is a gift). It will destroy itself when the time comes.

Attempting to 'do nothing' is a mental self-delusion ('doing' doing-nothing).

337 David Carse (who does not teach) gives the neo-advaitin view of how seeking appears to be going somewhere but isn't really: *"Spiritual seeking is the art of walking in very small circles. This does two things: it creates the illusion of motion, of getting*

somewhere; and it prevents one from stopping, from becoming still, which is where one would look around and see the futility of it all." (Ref. 7)

But, if direct self-knowledge is manifesting, the 'seeking' that is bringing this about cannot be futile from the standpoint of the seeker. And this self-knowledge is most unlikely to arise without prompting from a qualified teacher.

338 We do not know that we are already the Self and we have to go through the 'seeking' process in order to realize the truth. I must learn what I am not before I can realize who I am. For that, I need the benefit of teaching and, ideally, a teacher who can explain this to me; a teacher who knows how to use words as direct pointers, which can guide the mind to the direct realization of the truth (tat tvam asi). This process is the 'path' as perceived by traditional advaita.

(The claim that) Practice is of No Value

339   The Sanskrit word used for 'practice' is sAdhana, which refers to an activity carried out for some purpose, leading to some accomplishment or fulfillment - literally 'leading straight to the goal'. It is performed by a sAdhaka, usually translated as 'seeker' but the word as an adjective means 'productive of', 'accomplishing', 'fulfilling', 'perfecting'. What is achieved is sAdhya, 'that which is to be mastered or won', i.e. enlightenment.

340   Traditional teaching is therefore very clear that the seeker must practice if he wants to become enlightened. Shankara insisted that chatuShTaya sampatti was necessary to prepare the mind to gain the self-knowledge that will destroy the self-ignorance. The minds of most seekers are simply unable to see the truth of tat tvam asi (you are That) without preliminary study. (Note that, in practice in the present day, the 'mental preparation', teaching, and gaining of self-knowledge tend to happen simultaneously. Teachers do not normally require that a disciple serve them for thirty years before they condescend to pass on their wisdom!)

[sAdhana chatuShTaya sampatti is the fourfold pre-requisite specified by Shankara as needed by a seeker before he can achieve Self-realization. It is about acquiring the right attitude, learning self-control and discrimination etc. Contrary to the beliefs of many satsang seekers, mental outlook and behavior are relevant and important to cultivate receptivity to the teaching. Since enlightenment takes place in the mind, it is hardly unreasonable that the quality of the mind will be relevant.]

341   There is also a secondary aspect to this issue. According to traditional advaita, there are two elements to enlightenment. The first is enlightenment itself – j~nAna – wherein self-knowledge removes self-ignorance in the event of akhaNDAkAra vRRitti. The second is

87

the so-called fruits of knowledge (j~nAna phalam or jIvanmukta), which consist of those aspects that probably attracted the seeker in the first place, namely peace of mind, contentment, love, fearlessness etc. The teaching states that these benefits accrue to the seeker in proportion to the mental preparation that preceded enlightenment. It is possible to obtain j~nAna with some preparation but only the student who is fully prepared also gains jIvanmukta. Those students without any mental preparation at all gain neither. (Ref. 34) Furthermore, the mind of the jIvanmukti can be expected to mature further as subconscious material is resolved in the light of self-knowledge.

342   It follows from what has been said in the above sections that neo-advaitins deride all practices without exception.

343   Neo-advaitin teachers argue that, if practice could bring about enlightenment then the latter would be an *effect* of practice. Since reality is non-dual, this cannot be possible.

*This is to confuse paramArtha and vyavahAra again. The point is that ignorance, seeking, knowledge, enlightenment etc. are all at the level of the mind and vyavahAra. Cause and effect **do** operate at the level of the apparent world - and even the 'enlightened' switch on a kettle in order to make a cup of tea! Practice prepares the mind for gaining self-knowledge; knowledge removes ignorance; loss of self-ignorance is enlightenment - all within the apparent world of separate persons and duality.*

344   It is a paradox only when we confuse the ultimate reality with the apparent world.

345   Neo-advaitin teachers (and, increasingly, many satsang teachers) claim that practice takes us away from understanding who we are and that this understanding really requires no effort at all.

*As already noted, we do not have to do anything to 'gain' or 'become' the Self but something clearly does have to be done to enable the knowledge that we **are** the self to arise.*

346 Another neo-advaitin view is that practice maintains a belief that enlightenment is something that will be attained in the future; that it is therefore taking us away from what we already are.

*But this cannot be a problem so long as wrong ideas about 'who I am' are being removed, and the truth directly seen – ideas such as 'I am the body', for example. Indeed, until such time as these wrong ideas **are** removed, we are bound to remain bound.*

347 According to Vamadeva Shastri, Swami Sivananda once said, concerning the need for practice: *"Without preparing ourselves through preliminary practices, the only answer to the question 'Who am I?' is 'The same old fool.'"* (Ref. 43)

348 The neo-advaitin claims that no mental preparation is needed.

An example that can help us to understand that it is the traditional viewpoint that is correct is that of Newton's apple. If we are not prepared, we will not be able to recognize the truth when it falls on our head, metaphorically speaking. This is why many seekers continue to attend satsangs given by neo-teachers and repeatedly hear the truth yet continually fail to appreciate it.

*[As stated elsewhere, most satsang teachers simply state the truth rather than using a proven methodology to lead the student from where they are **to** the recognition of that truth. Both elements are needed in the teaching situation.]*

349 But, since enlightenment is effectively an event in the mind, it follows that the mind has to be 'ready' for this event – hence the

need for mental preparation and discipline.

350 The mere fact that only a few people become seekers shows that there must be something that differentiates them from 'normal' people! What is usually the case is that such a person has come to the realization that happiness cannot be gained from any of the traditionally advertised sources. This in itself effectively constitutes a mental preparation but clearly much more is needed before direct knowledge may be gained.

But many of those attending satsang have still not realized that happiness is not to be found in duality – they think that satsang will provide it! Needless, to say, it cannot.

351 If the understanding is not already of a certain level of maturity, the teaching will not be appreciated.

Swami Parthasarathy uses the metaphor of a very young child offered the choice between a bar of chocolate or a $100 bill. He understands the instant gratification that the chocolate will bring but does not yet appreciate that the money can purchase many bars in the future and so he chooses the chocolate. This is an example of how discrimination (viveka) grows as we mature.

352 Nevertheless, the claim that we do not have to do anything obviously makes satsang/neo-advaita attractive and traditional unattractive, especially to the Western mind.

If seekers believed that a long period of organized, mental training was needed, they would be unlikely to attend occasional satsang with different teachers. Satsangs flourish as a result of the mistaken belief that anyone can go to a satsang and the 'penny is likely to drop' there and then.

353 Neo-advaitins claim that seeking (or not) is just part of the story. *But the ego cannot really believe this and it is egos who attend satsang. Of course, egos frequently delude themselves and so the claim is a great ego-booster! (This may also happen with traditional seekers but traditional teaching acknowledges the existence of the ego and the problems it creates, whereas neo-advaita does not.)*

354 The teaching methods of traditional and satsang/neo will be addressed in separate sections below but a few examples are given here.

355 Reading books, especially scriptures, is accorded a lower status in Traditional teaching than is hearing those same words from a qualified guru. Indeed, the original tradition was purely oral – shruti means 'heard' – and there were once no books to be read. It is, nevertheless, regarded as an extremely worthwhile pursuit, although ideally as part of a formal course of teaching rather than in isolation (anyone who has attempted to read the Upanishads in an uncommented form will know that they are far from easy reading!)

356 It must be pointed out, too, that many of those teachers who state that reading is a waste of time nevertheless continue to publish books of their own.

357 Ramana Maharshi is frequently cited by satsang teachers as an example of someone who 'realized himself' without the need for traditional teaching or scriptures.

What is disregarded however, by many students and teachers is the question of mental readiness, as has already been discussed. It is simply not the case that everyone is equal as far as preparedness for realization is concerned. (We are all brahman in paramArtha but there are fools and sages in vyavahAra.) Whether or not it is believed that some have acquired their mental clarity and discrimi-

91

nation etc. in previous lives is beside the point. The fact remains that some are ready whilst others must discipline the mind first through possibly many years (or lifetimes) of practice.

358 Robert Adams commented: *"It is true that some people have become enlightened without doing anything. Those people are far and few between. It's better not to take a chance, and to practice rather than continue your life the way it is and wait. For you may wait incarnation after incarnation after incarnation."* (Ref. 58)

359 Recognizing that the Self which you truly are is always unchangingly present, while everything else comes and goes and is subject to time, is a key practice in Traditional teaching and most satsang teachers would perhaps acknowledge this. Neo-advaitin teachers, however, claim that this is irrelevant – there is no one to be 'in the present'.

360 The negative attitude of neo-advaitins to practice follows from their insistence that there is no person and no such thing as free will. E.g. one cannot choose to give attention, for example. There is no one to choose. The neo-advaitin would say that 'attention happens'.

361 Some satsang teachers argue that any effort is counter-productive, strengthening the ego, inculcating pride etc. Chuck Hillig (a non-traditional writer/teacher) says that *"All fervent attempts to control or to mortify this illusory ego through penance, rituals and sacrifice, however, will only serve to intensify the delusion that this ego is actually very real and that it only needs to be, somehow, subdued, conquered or destroyed."* (Ref. 20)

But this is to misunderstand the nature and purpose of preparation. 'Rituals and sacrifices' etc. are a part of karma kANDa (the first part of the Vedas) and nothing to do with advaita and the mind needs to be stilled and controlled if it is to be able to hear the teaching and allow direct knowledge to arise.

362 Ramesh Balsekar makes similar statements: *"The disciple thinks that it is the acquisition of knowledge which will get rid of the ignorance while the guru knows that ignorance is itself the result of the positive action of identification. Any further positive action on the part of the illusory individual, such as any practices or disciplines, would only make the identification stronger."* (From 'The Duet of One', quoted in Ref. 32)

Both of these statements suggest that he is confusing indirect and direct knowledge – see 36 - 37 where Shankara makes precisely this point, namely that no action is required in order to obtain direct knowledge.

363 And Tony Parsons says that: *"Doctrines, processes and progressive paths which seek enlightenment only exacerbate the problems they address by reinforcing the idea that the apparent self can find something it presumes it has lost. It is that very effort, that investment in self-identity, that continuously recreates the illusion of separation from oneness"* (Ref. 36)

364 But this is to misunderstand the problem and solution. No amount of effort will enable us to wake from the dream that is mAyA; only loss of self-ignorance can achieve this. But traditional teaching will only have this effect in a mind that is ready to accept it. It is for this mental preparation that effort is required. (Also, the teaching nowhere assumes that we have 'lost the self'.)

365 John Wheeler says that: *"You do not need to practice to be what you are."* (Ref. 16) and goes on to say that: *"Once the mind gets hold of the notions of awakening or liberation, there is invariably an attempt to turn this into some kind of goal, which the individual hopes to attain."*

Both statements can be accepted as true. The mistake is to link the two. Practice in the traditional sense does not relate to the mind trying to achieve enlightenment but to mental preparation. Self-knowledge can only be gained in a mind which is relatively calm and peaceful. When the self-knowledge occurs, there is no practice involved; its happening is inevitable. There is not, in any case, anything seriously wrong with the individual having the goal of enlightenment. The misunderstanding associated with this is probably inevitable and will naturally be resolved by a good teacher.

366   Swami Chinmayananda says that the objective is to remove the ignorance, after which the self-luminous knowledge shines forth. He says *"the clouds are to be removed; the sun does not need to be illumined."* (Ref. 60)

367   Alan Jacobs (president of the Ramana Maharshi Foundation in the UK) also argues against the idea that practice reinforces the ego: *"The argument often put against sAdhanA by many teachers, that it strengthens the ego, is false. Surrender and Self-enquiry are designed to undermine and eventually destroy the conditioned and inborn tendencies (vAsanA-s) as well as the narcissistic parts of the ego."* (Ref. 38)

368   This attitude reflects that given in the Kaivalya Upanishad (I.11). There, the metaphor of fire and wood is used - one which was particularly popular with Ramana Maharshi. The verse is translated by Swami Parthasarathy as follows: *"Having made the individual the (lower) piece of wood and OM the upper piece of wood, through churning by sustained practice of knowledge the wise burn the bond (of ignorance)."* (Ref. 70). In the case of the wood, both the fuel and the resultant fire are 'contained' in the wood itself - all that is required to manifest the fire is friction. Similarly, Atman is 'contained' within the jIva along with the 'fuel' of the vAsanA-s.

94

Practice is the 'friction' that brings the fire of the Atman into manifestation and, in doing so, destroys the vAsanA-s.

369 Neo-advaitins argue that the methods of traditional advaita support rather than undermine the ego whereas neo-advaita sees through the person as an illusion. In this context, the metaphor of setting a thief to catch a thief is sometimes used – the ego can never conquer the ego.

But the person, in the sense of a body-mind organism is not an illusion – it is mithyA. It also seems likely that much of their criticism is based upon a lack of clear understanding of the traditional methods.

370 Finally, those teachers who deprecate any form of practice fail to explain why regular attendance of their satsangs is not itself a form of practice.

Need for a guru

371 The Katha Upanishad states: *"When taught by a man of inferior understanding, this Atman cannot be truly known, even though frequently thought upon. There is no way (to know It) unless it is taught by another (an illumined teacher), for it is subtler than the subtle and beyond argument."* (I.2.8) (Ref. 82)

372 The problem with simply reading the scriptures or the words of a sage is that, although we may question what has been written, based upon our own particular nature, upbringing, education and previous reading, we have only those same words to provide an answer. If the question is asked of a guru, we are able to receive different words, biased towards our own particular difficulty. Such questioning may continue indefinitely until a satisfactory understanding is obtained. A good teacher may even intuit our problems before we are able clearly to formulate them.

Swami Chinmayananda was asked why we can't simply study Vedanta ourselves in the library. He answered: "Ask that question to the library." (Ref. 35)

373 Many of the words in the scriptures are not meant in their literal, dualistic sense at all but as pointers to the non-dual. In the absence of a teacher who understands this, the reader will have no access at all to the intended meaning.

374 Furthermore, the scriptures are rarely couched in a clear and unambiguous way. They were, after all, intended to be spoken and then explained, rather than simply read. They should really be 'unfolded' by a teacher who is enlightened, who understands them in depth and can use them as they were intended – namely to point to the reality and not simply to be interpreted literally. They were never meant to be studied on one's own, prior to gaining

Knowledge.

375 Lastly, the scriptures were written hundreds or, in some case, thousands of years ago in an obscure language (Sanskrit) and in the context of an alien society. It is scarcely surprising that they are often difficult to interpret. A Westerner with no specialized knowledge is unlikely to be able to derive the intended meaning from them without the assistance of a shrotriya who can reinterpret the words in a modern context.

376 Shankara states that both the scripture and a teacher are necessary. In his commentary on the Bhagavad Gita (II.21), he states that: *"The mind, refined by shama and dama – i.e. by the subjugation of the body, the mind and the senses – and equipped with the teachings of the Scripture and the teacher, constitutes the sense by which the Self may be seen."* (Ref. 87) He is even more specific in his commentary on the Brihadaranyaka Upanishad (II.5.15): *"those alone who follow both scripture and teachers transcend ignorance."* (quoted in Ref. 84)

[Note that shama and dama, mental discipline and control of the senses, are two of the shamAdi ShaTka sampatti or 'six qualities' that form part of Shankara's chatuShTaya sampatti.]

377 The 'progress' of a seeker should ideally be constantly monitored by a teacher. Problems and misunderstandings can then be resolved and advice may be given. In this way, the seeker may avoid straying into further confusion and, instead, the way may be pointed towards full realization of the truth.

378 We need a teacher to enable us to assimilate objective knowledge (otherwise we would have libraries but no universities). This is especially so in the case of spiritual knowledge, which relates to the subject and cannot be known or studied in any objective sense.

Swami Dayananda puts it thus: "Words must be elaborately defined so that what is meant is what is received. Paradoxes must be juggled, illustrations handled, and contexts set up so that the implied meanings can be seen. For this a teacher is necessary, because he knows the truth as well as the methodology for revealing it." (Ref. 52)

379 Not only is a teacher able to answer our particular doubts, as and when they arise (rather than our having to spend a long time trying to find the answers in books or on the Internet!), he or she is able to raise doubts that may not even have occurred to us, and answer those too.

380 The guru-disciple relationship is a long-term affair. Each student will have his or her own specific difficulties in understanding. Only over a period of time can the teacher come to understand these fully and then systematically assist in their resolution.

381 There is a story in the yoga vAsiShTha that explains why a guru is needed, although he does not directly bring about enlightenment: *"It concerns a miser who loses a small coin whilst he is walking in the forest. Worried that the loss of this will incur further losses through inability to invest it, he spends three days searching for it. He fails to find it but, instead, finds a jewel. Clearly it was the miserliness of the man and his determination to recover this small coin that led to his finding something truly valuable. In the same way, it is said that the disciple, having been instructed by the guru, spends all his time searching for something. He thinks that the search is for something for himself – peace of mind, meaning in his life or whatever. But he fails to find this. Instead, if he perseveres, he finds something of much greater value – his true Self."* (Ref. 2) It is the guidance and encouragement of the guru that spurs the seeker on to his or her final destination.

382 The stereotypical idea of the guru in the West is not one of a revered sage, possibly since the concept itself first gained general currency in the sixties with its 'free love' and drugs. Even today, many people think that a guru is someone of dubious morals who dupes the unsuspecting disciple. This is in marked contrast to the attitude towards sages and saMnyAsin-s in the east, where they are treated with respect and deference.

It would also be true to say that there will always be charlatans, ready to take advantage of a susceptible seeker, in both East and West.

383 Since neo-advaitin teachers believe that any sort of practice is futile, it follows that they also claim that there is no need for, or value in, a guru.

Nevertheless, they themselves continue to hold satsangs and residential courses around the country, and many of those attending are habitual followers.

384 We need a guru to help us dispel the self-ignorance. Ramana Maharshi explains: *"The guru does not bring about Self-Realization. He simply removes the obstacles to it. The Self is always realized."* (Ref. 28) [Note that he actually means that the Self is always *free*.]

385 The Chandogya Upanishad (Ch. 6, section XV, verses 1 to 2) uses the metaphor of someone who has been blindfolded and left in the middle of a forest. There is no way that he can find his way out without help. The guru is the one who provides 'pointers' – e.g. "walk in this direction until you reach a large tree that has been struck by lightning, then turn east and proceed until you reach the river" etc. *"Even thus a man who has a duly qualified teacher learns (his way) and thus remains liberated (from all worldly ties)*

till he attains (the Truth – mokSha)" (Ref. 83)

One always reaches a destination more quickly with a guide than when attempting to find the way oneself, especially in the jungle.

386   That 'I am' is self-evident and to know this requires no teacher. That 'I am brahman' is not initially self-evident and, in order to understand it, vichAra (investigation) is needed. The answer is given by the shruti but simply reading them is most unlikely to provide the necessary comprehension and conviction. It is rarely possible to see beyond that which we already know. Someone who is established in that knowledge is the best person to explain it to us.

387   In satsang, the words of the 'teacher' arise in response to questions asked by the 'seeker' – this is obviously an apparent duality but is the natural working of cause and effect in vyavahAra. This process of question and answer is usually called 'teaching' but neo-advaitins deny that they are doing this.

388   Neo-advaitins may concede that a teacher is useful in that there is less chance of the seeker deluding herself that she has understood the message of written material. With a live interaction, the various 'mind games' can be exposed (not always in a sympathetic way).

389   As before, the views of most satsang teachers are probably intermediate between the clear guidance from tradition that a guru is necessary and the hard-line neo-advaitin view that one is not. Thus John Wheeler's concern is that they should not *"encourage the seeker to engage in protracted processes that subtly support the idea that understanding is in the future or the result of practice."* He says that *"the best teachers point out that this understanding is immediate and available, here and now."* (Ref. 16)

*It should, however, be made clear that the knowledge may **not** come* *until sometime in the future. Again there is a danger of confusing the fact that I am already the Self with the equally likely fact that I do not yet know this.*

390 Many sources state that the only 'true' guru is already within oneself (so-called sadguru - a 'good teacher' - sat means 'true' or 'real').

391 Thus, Ramana Maharshi said that: *"So long as one thinks of himself as little, he must take hold of the great - the guru; he must not however look upon the guru as a person; the Sage is never other than the real Self of the disciple. When that Self is realized then there is neither guru nor disciple."* (Ref. 31)

392 The sense of this is that, upon realization, it is understood that the essence of seeker and guru is one and the same. It is also this truth that perhaps leads the neo-advaitins to claim that the act of seeking out a guru, and all this entails, to some degree propagates the very idea of dualism that we are trying to destroy.

But, although the teacher knows that both are the same, the seeker initially does not – this is why the teacher is needed. When the seeker knows it too, she is enlightened.

393 Alan Jacobs who, in his role as chairman of the Ramana Maharshi Foundation UK, met and became friendly with many of the Western satsang teachers, suggests that most of these teachers are by no means 'sages' and says that: *"I am sure they are too honest ever to make such a claim and would all agree with this thesis."* (Ref. 38)

His suggestion is that, although they may have had genuine enlightenment 'experiences', they still have active vAsanA-s and thus are only in the early stages of evolution to 'Sagedom'. But, as pointed out in 216 - 217, enlightenment has nothing to do with experiences.

394 The danger of a false guru is brilliantly put by David Carse: *"When the blind lead the blind, none of the followers can see that the leader himself carries a white cane."* (Ref. 7)

The scriptures also use this image: "Living in the midst of ignorance and deeming themselves intelligent and enlightened, the ignorant go round and round staggering in crooked paths, like the blind led by the blind." Katha Upanishad I.2.5 (Ref. 98)

395 Swami Paramarthananda also uses this metaphor. He says that the seeker looking for a guru is like a blind man holding on to another to lead him. If it turns out that he, too, is blind, the likelihood of falling over is doubled. (Ref. 34)

396 And Jed McKenna (a non-traditional teacher/writer) points out that, just because a particular guru is popular, this does not necessarily make him or her good: *"Popularity among the soundly asleep may not be the best criterion by which to judge a method for waking up."* (Ref. 10)

397 It is the true teacher who will help dissolve the ignorance. The ego of the seeker may effectively desire a false teacher, who will elevate his 'spiritual self' but in the end poses no threat to who he believes himself to be.

Traditional Teaching

Format

398   Traditional teaching identifies practices and a 'path' that will help the student towards enlightenment.

399   The process can be considered to have three elements, all of which are necessary: a) the scriptures as the pramANa; b) the seeker, together with his or her own experience and reasoning faculties; c) the guru, who brings the first two elements together using his own direct knowledge and skillful interpretation of the words. As William Cenkner puts it: *"The guru establishes continuity between scripture and reason. He calls forth the experience of the student to test and verify whatever is taught by himself or scripture."* (Ref. 84)

400   The teaching is gradual, leading students gently from where they are, with all of their mistaken views of themselves and the world, to the final truth of non-duality. It acknowledges the starting point of desires, identification etc. and aims to educate, undermining these concepts and eliminating them one by one. Traditional advaita tells us something we can accept that will enable us to revise our previous stance and move forwards.

The best traditional teaching brings revelations of understanding while most of the neo-advaitin teaching remains alien to our direct experience. It is a case of 'Aah!' versus 'uh?'

401   Advaita states that the ultimate, unmanifest reality is non-dual and without limits or attributes. It cannot, therefore, be spoken of directly. Lest this be misunderstood, however, this does *not* mean that it cannot be spoken of at all.

As an example, the Kena Upanishad tells us that: "It is the ear of the ear, the mind of the mind, the speech of the speech, the life of the life, the eye of the eye." (I.2) and: "That which speech does not illumine, but which illumines speech..." (I.4) (Ref. 82)

402   Traditional advaita employs proven procedures or prakriyA-s which remove misunderstandings and point to actual truths. These provide explanations etc. using a sustained, logical, stepwise approach.

403   This is a significant undertaking, expected to take many years (if not lifetimes).

404   Teachers defer to the scriptures as the ultimate authority for that knowledge which is not available via our usual means of perception. Traditional teachers have read and fully understood the scriptures (have become shrotriya-s) and usually utilize them for teaching, 'unfolding' them to the student. The method of argument is supremely logical, having originated with Gautama and the naiyAyika philosophers in the 3rd century CE, and this logic also forms part of the teaching.

405   The teaching makes frequent use of Sanskrit terminology. There is good reason for this, namely that there are often no corresponding words available in English. Even when there are, the specific nuances are best conveyed by using a word which is not already known to the student. If a common English word is used, the concept is likely to be unexamined because thought to be already understood.

*Satsang teachers, especially those of neo-advaitin persuasion, usually claim that Sanskrit terminology is redundant and are often themselves unfamiliar with the terms. Consequently, the advaitin concepts are frequently misunderstood to have their familiar meaning. (E.g. 'bliss' – the usual translation of Ananda – is equated with 'ecstasy'.) It is, however, true that Vedanta **can** be taught without using any Sanskrit, providing that the teacher has complete* *understanding of the methodology.*

Preparation

406 The mind needs to be prepared in many ways to be able to receive and recognize the truth. A mind which is still pointing outward toward the creation, expecting that solutions can be found there, is a mind which is not yet ready to recognize the truth. In ancient times, the teacher would not accept a student unless eligibility (adhikAra), in terms of moral and psychological readiness could be demonstrated. (Ref. 84)

407 The practices of karma yoga (the yoga of action) and bhakti yoga (devotion) may be regarded as 'secondary' sAdhanA-s, which have the end result of stilling the mind and making it more receptive to the 'primary' practice of j~nAna yoga (the yoga of knowledge), using the techniques of shravaNa etc. (see 355).

408 Traditionally, a seeker must want enlightenment (mumukShutva – see 308)

409 The seeker needs to give up the desire for objects, etc. This is the idea of renunciation – we give up our earlier desire for those 'things' which are never going to bring lasting happiness. But this does not mean that we give up our comforts and become saMnyAsin-s, living in the open and begging our food as traditionally happened in India. It simply means that material aspects assume reduced importance now, replaced by the overriding goal of obtaining self-knowledge.

This practice is derided by neo-advaitins as the 'desire to renounce desire' and, indeed, renunciation cannot really be enforced but should be a natural 'falling away' of previous desires as they are supplanted by the higher desire for truth.

410 The traditional seeker is searching for the truth, not greater pleasure; finding a 'meaning' to his or her life, avoiding death etc. The teaching inculcates viveka and vairAgya, so that we may differentiate between the real and unreal. Those things that do not lead to the former then no longer hold any attraction. Many satsang teachers feel they have 'succeeded' if the seeker goes away happy but the true purpose of the teacher is to undermine the seeker's belief that he or she exists as a separate entity.

411 The 'aim' of traditional teaching is to cause the seeker to realize that the 'innate Self', Atman, is identical with the 'universal Self', brahman. This message is the essence of the shruti.

Modern teachers usually claim simply that our aim is to 'realize the Self' or to 'understand our true nature'.

Need for provisional truths

412 The traditional teaching of advaita embodies stages in understanding, adapted to each student's situation, and these are transcended one by one. The seeker will probably initially be fully bound up in life's complexities. Over a period of time, the various levels of identification will be undermined and new understanding gained. Each new idea must be heard, reflected upon and progressively assimilated, before the full implications may be appreciated. As aspects are revisited, new insights are gained.

Simply stating the conclusions will never bring about these same results instantaneously. To this extent, it could be said that traditional advaita has a clear teaching methodology, in which satsang plays a valid role. Western satsang teaching has no methodology at all; it simply takes the satsang out of context and tries to use it on its own.

413 In particular, traditional advaita quite deliberately employs dualistic

teachings. These include such concepts as karma (and reincarnation), interpreted through the practice of the yoga of action (karma yoga), and the existence of gods and worship, interpreted through the practice of bhakti yoga. Such teaching methods are utilized by the teacher according to the particular needs and abilities of each student. They are neither unnecessary nor optional.

414   In his teachings on the Mandukya Upanishad (Ref. 34), Swami Paramarthananda uses several analogies to help explain why such strategies are needed. The first is the example of school. We all usually accept that we must go to school in order to learn the various subjects which will benefit us in life. All good students recognize the value of school as preparation for the adult world. But no one would want to stay in school for their entire life. Once the examinations have proved our ability, we move into the 'real' world and begin to use the knowledge that has been gained. Nevertheless, no one in their right mind would say that, since we are going to have to go into the world anyway eventually, there is therefore no point in going to school at all.

415   The next two examples are even more apposite. The first is the one of the pole vault. We need the pole in order to push ourselves up to the bar. Admittedly we have to let go of it in the end but it would be stupid to say that, since we are not taking it with us, we might as well not use it in the first place.

416   The second is the example of scaffolding. We must use this when building a house, even though it is eventually discarded. It is most unlikely that any house we tried to build without it would withstand the buffeting of the first storm. Thus it is hardly surprising that seekers, who have been 'taught' using the neo-advaitin 'method', find themselves in serious trouble at the first signs of an upheaval in their lives. We only remove the scaffolding once the building has adequate self-support.

417   All of these illustrate why it is that the initial, dualistic teaching of advaita is needed by most students. Such teaching only has provisional validity but, without it, the seeker will never reach the final understanding.

418   Furthermore, the fact that some students need initial 'stepping stones' explains why the satsang 'one size for all' method could only ever be partially successful. If you need a particular stone and it is not provided, you are going to fall into the river and may even drown! Only when a teacher has a prolonged and close association with the student are the particular needs going to be appreciated. You cannot give the same advice to all students.

Some traditional methods (prakriyA-s)

419   What is taught often provides only an interim explanation which helps to resolve a more deep-rooted misunderstanding.

420   The key method is called adhyAropa-apavAda - expounding principles and theories, which are later retracted once they have served their purpose of removing some mistaken identification or mental block (adhyAropa means erroneously attributing one thing to another, though quite deliberately in this case on the part of the teacher; apavAda means denial or contradiction). [Note that this does not mean that the final truths are reserved or held back until the student is ready but that, as basic understanding grows, more sophisticated explanations can be given.]

This technique has also been described as 'using a thorn to remove a thorn'.

421   Reality (or satyam) is non-dual and consequently all that there is. All of the separate appearances of bodies and objects are mithyA.

422   When all of the mistaken views have been taken away, the truth

stands revealed. It was there all the time, merely covered over.

423 Another classic method utilizes a similar approach. dRRigdRRishya viveka means to discriminate between the seer and the seen. We perceive the body as an object; we are aware of our thoughts and sense organs etc. Whoever 'we' are, we cannot be these things which are seen as objects; we have to be the ultimate witness (subject) of all objects. I remain unchanging while everything else changes.

424 Such methods are primarily 'negating' techniques – we are 'not that' – and, at the end, we are left with 'who-we-are' and 'things-which-we-are-not'. This is obviously not non-duality. If these were the only techniques used, it would not be clear what it is exactly that remains after all-that-we-are-not has been negated.

425 Accordingly, traditional teaching also utilizes positive pointers to our real nature. Normally, the words that we use when we talk about something describe attributes of the object. Brahman is not an object, it is the subject, so this is not possible; all definitions would necessarily be objective and therefore 'not I'. Instead, the scriptures give pointers (lakShaNa-s) to the essential nature (svarUpa) of brahman (see 401 for example).

426 Initially the seeker believes herself to be an entity separate from the non-dual reality. The mahAvAkya 'tat tvam asi' tells us that there is no separation. The technique of bhAga tyAga lakShaNa cancels out the apparent contradictions between 'little me' and 'big brahman' and leaves the simple equivalence.

The technique is best explained by example:

"Suppose that you and a friend, A, both went to school with a third person, X. Although you were not particularly friendly with X, you

knew him quite well but, since leaving school you lost touch and have forgotten all about him. Today, you happen to be walking along with A and see Y, who is a famous film star, walking by on the other side of the street. You have seen films starring Y and admire him very much. A now makes some comment such as 'Y has come a long way in the world since we knew him, hasn't he?' You are mystified, since you have never even spoken to Y as far as you know, and you ask A to explain himself. A then makes the revelatory statement: Y is that X whom we knew at school. All of the contradictory aspects, that X is an insignificant, scruffy, spotty youth that you once knew at school, while Y is a rich, famous and talented actor, are all cancelled out, leaving the bare equation that X and Y are the same person. Furthermore, the knowledge is aparokSha - immediate. We do not have to study the reasoning or meditate upon it for a long time." (Ref. 2)

427 Another reason why we have difficulty using words to describe our absolute nature is that words usually have opposites. Thus, some teachers might speak of our nature being 'love' but our dualistic experience also recognizes 'hate'. In order to use words to point to a non-dual reality, any duality of the words must be transcended. Thus, for example, if we speak of absolute 'knowledge', that has to be understood as not just the knowing of facts but the knowing of both knowledge and ignorance themselves. In this way, the mind is pointed towards the non-duality of the subject and the resolution of the apparently dualistic objects.

428 The subject, me, is that in which all of these appearances arise. Having negated the appearances (those things of which I am aware) the teaching points back to me with words such as anantam – unlimited. Everything else constantly changes while I remain the changeless witness of all.

429 Because the words that are used are contrary to our everyday

experience, the rationale has to be conveyed somehow. Traditional advaita provides techniques for doing this. One of them is called arundhatI nyAya. arundhatI is the Indian name given to a star, Alcor, in the constellation of Ursa Major (Great Bear, Plough or Big Dipper); nyAya means logical argument. In marriage ceremonies in India, the star is pointed out to the bride as an example to be followed, since the star is 'devoted' to its companion star, Mizar or vAsiShTha (arundhatI was the wife of vAsiShTha). Because the star is scarcely visible, it is necessary to lead the eye to it gradually. Thus one might first locate the constellation by reference to the moon. Then the attention can be directed to the bright star that is at the tail of the Great Bear. Finally, there is a companion star which is only 11 minutes distant and fourth magnitude that can only be seen by people with exceptional eyesight. This is arundhatI. (Ref. 2)

430 This is the technique used in the Taittiriya Upanishad for the classic metaphor of the five sheaths that 'cover up' our real nature. This suggests first that we are the gross body (made of food), that we can easily see, but then points towards increasingly more subtle aspects until we can appreciate the 'core' essence.

431 Words such as knowledge, existence, consciousness, bliss are used to point towards my true nature. Having negated everything else, there is only my Self left to give these words meaning. It is in this way that traditional teaching effectively uses words to explain to us that which is beyond words. Without the skillful use of the relevant methods, the essentially dualistic nature of language will never be transcended.

Criticism

432 Traditional methods are regarded as archaic and no longer relevant to a modern age by many satsang teachers and all neo-advaitins.

But you can't replace an established and proven methodology with *a complete absence of any method. Furthermore, although times, society and people change, the basic problems do not. Hence, the old teachings will always essentially still be applicable. They do not need to change because they already work and have been proven over many centuries. (Why, in any case, would it only be **now** that it needs to change? Shankara systematized the already-existing philosophy in the 8th Century. Is it only now that people, society etc. have changed?) [However, note 375.]*

433   In fact, rather than society having evolved such that these teachings are no longer needed, it would be more accurate to say that they are now needed more than ever.

434   Traditional teaching is accused of being a 'religion' with dogma and indoctrination. And religions are thought to be outdated; only for the naïve.

*Advaita **is** a religion in the literal sense of the word ('binding back' – Latin 're-ligare' - to the truth). So is neo-advaita! There is also dogma in traditional advaita – 'principle or set of principles laid down by an authority as incontrovertibly true' (Oxford English Dictionary). But advaita could never be accused of indoctrination; it is always emphasized that one should not take what is said by the teacher as necessarily true but should reflect upon it and verify what has been said from one's own experience.*

435   The idea that traditional teaching is invalid, and the consequential growth of the Western satsang approach to teaching, appears to have begun with Sri Poonja.

One of his disciples, Pratima, explains: "Papaji's message is simplicity itself. Nothing to attain anew, only a thin veil to be removed. He is totally revolutionary in this. The traditional paths of seeking the truth all seem so laborious and painstaking... maybe in

10 or 20 years or so or at the moment of death we will realize who we are all along! So why not wake up now! Why waste time?" (Ref. 21) For most seekers, however, the veil is probably thicker than they would like to admit!

436 The seeker might well ask why it is that a sampradAya teacher should be better or more worthy of listening to than the independent teacher. The answer is simple – authority (in the sense of proven to work) and training. Why should one pay more attention to the claims of one 'ordinary person' than another? If a totally unqualified teacher says 'This is it' and my own experience tells me that 'no it isn't', who is right? Should I not give more credence to first-hand experience? On the other hand, if a teacher is able to say 'this is what my teacher told me' and so on, back down a noble line of sages to the shruti itself, then *that* is worthy of attending to.

It might be said that the traditional path is a well-worn one and we are therefore far less likely to stray, whereas the neo-advaitin path is, by its own admission, no path at all.

Satsang Teaching

History

437 Ramana Maharshi was 'self-taught' and thus all of those teachers claiming him as their guru are without any backing tradition. Furthermore, Ramana never trained his disciples to be teachers, as opposed to what happens within a traditional sampradAya, where the communicated knowledge is likened to one candle flame lighting another - the same flame, the same knowledge, the same teaching, the same pramANa.

438 Ramana's story therefore effectively legitimized the idea of 'independent' teachers, who could claim enlightenment without the authentication of a formal, traditional guru.

One wonders what he would have thought of the frequent use of his photograph by many modern teachers, implying a spurious endorsement.

439 Nisargadatta Maharaj, though belonging to a formal sampradAya (the Navnath or Inchgiri tradition) also held regular meetings to cater for all of the transient Westerners travelling to India to seek him out. Again, many of those who attended his meetings are now themselves teaching, although the formal sampradAya seems to have ended with Nisargadatta Maharaj and Ranjit Maharaj. Western style satsang teaching now prevails amongst his disciples.

Format

440 The 'method' of most satsang teachers involves answering a few random questions (this also applies to most of their books).

These questions are essentially 'personal' so that answers will not necessarily be relevant to many attendees. They are also inevitably random so that it is rarely possible for a satsang to address a particular topic in a systematic and exhaustive manner.

441 Most questions are also about finding happiness in the seeker's own life and not about advaita at all. Until the seeker recognizes that happiness is not to be found 'out there', there will be no progress.

442 Jed McKenna says about questions from seekers: *"Students aren't really qualified to ask questions and if I simply answered the questions they felt the need to ask then they'd only manage to deepen their own entrenchment in their false beliefs."* (Ref. 10) Cynical though this might sound, it is not unreasonable. Within traditional teaching, students don't usually ask questions out of context but only in relation to scripture that has just been unfolded (or to a topic which is being investigated as part of the ongoing teaching). In such a case it will be both pertinent and relevant to other members of the class.

443 Meeting sizes vary. Those of the more popular teachers, such as Adyashanti, may be several hundred. In such a situation, the opportunity for asking a question will be much reduced. A seeker may easily be too embarrassed to speak in front of so many people. Even at small gatherings, one particular student may dominate all of the time available for questions.

444 Some attendees ask questions merely in order to be the center of attention. Consequently, it is normal for topics not to be investigated in any depth before someone changes the subject.

445 And some attendees never ask questions because they are afraid of being the center of attention. Unless their questions happen to be asked coincidentally by someone else, they are most unlikely to resolve their misunderstandings.

446 Most seekers will typically attend satsangs by a number of different

teachers, usually whichever one happens to be in their area. Consequently, a seeker is likely to hear varied, and possibly even conflicting, answers to what may be apparently the same question. Attempts to reconcile these will probably lead to greater confusion.

This is why traditionally one is advised to find and stay with a single teacher.

447 Traditionally, seekers expected a long and dedicated (though eventful and rewarding) journey, which might involve studying with a guru for many years. These days, people want the answers now, not when their mind is prepared genuinely to understand them. Accordingly, teaching styles have developed to try to cater for this demand – attempting to convey the essential truth in a two-hour satsang or a weekend 'intensive'.

448 The intermittent, noncommittal approach of Western satsang teaching cannot provide the necessary individual, contextual and stepwise approach.

449 Satsang teaching usually cannot teach individual students. Attendees are 'transients' and there is insufficient time for a teacher to get to know their idiosyncrasies. Therefore, what teachers say at satsangs may or may not be relevant to most listeners and may not even be relevant to the questioner. Transcribed satsangs are even worse, of course, since the complete context is often lacking.

450 Satsangs are inevitably mixed ability, some seekers being relatively new to the 'scene' while others are long-term seekers with considerable knowledge (or considerable confusion, depending on the source of that knowledge). It is not possible to provide answers to suit all levels, with the clear danger that they will suit no one.

451 More specifically, satsang and neo-advaitin teaching may claim to

be suitable for all 'levels' of seeker, i.e. to be democratic as opposed to the extreme 'mystical' teachings which were only given following a seeker's long preparation and initiation. Traditional teaching takes neither of these extreme positions but recognizes the need for mental preparation before being able to appreciate the more subtle aspects. Consequently, for example, a traditional teacher would not attempt to teach the Mandukya Upanishad to seekers who had not already studied the simpler ones.

452 Satsang teaching may provide a useful introduction to the *idea* of non-duality...

...but no introduction to the correct teaching of it and no foundation of understanding for later clarity.

453 Because the satsang approach does not provide any background understanding of non-duality, satsang attendees may not learn anything at all.

The cynic might also note that satsangs require no preparation, whereas studying and preparing to present a series of talks on an Upanishad, for example, might take many months if not years.

454 Satsang may help to undermine intellectual preconceptions, ahaMkAra etc. but the same danger applies.

455 It is inevitable that, to some degree, satsangs are aimed at 'satis-fying' the demands of the attendee. There is certainly a 'quality' spectrum, from the most materialistic to the most spiritual but there is an inescapable element of commercial transaction when money changes hands. In a 'supply and demand' situation, those satsangs which 'succeed' are the ones that give the attendee what he or she wants. Accordingly, if what most want is a sociable gathering to discuss psychological problems, or a positive or pleasurable

experience, that is likely to be what they end up getting, as opposed to a clear exposition on the subject of advaita.

456   It is as though the style and content of current satsangs is a parallel evolution to satisfy the requirements of the 'evolved' individual. The prolonged, in-depth, possibly lifelong teaching has been condensed and distilled into something that can be covered in a two-hour session. The message has now been reduced to an almost content-less 'This is it!' - a high-energy message, low in spiritual nourishment; the 'fast food' of non-dual teaching.

But, unfortunately, there are no short-cuts and attempts to bypass the logical, step by step development of traditional methods are extremely unlikely to lead to the desired result. Far more likely is that additional confusion will be caused, which will have to be removed later before the proper teaching can begin.

Psychology

457   Most seekers go to satsangs because they are dissatisfied with their lives and want to be 'happy'. Many satsang teachers reinforce the belief that being vitally in the moment and living life to the full is the aim of spiritual seeking. But the aim of traditional advaita is to realize the Self, not to gain a better saMsAra. Only removal of self-ignorance can bring true fulfillment (by enabling us to see that we are already full-filled).

458   Those seekers who are insecure and are looking to find security through relationships with others are also misguided. Relationships are only possible in duality and, indeed, another name for the Self-knowledge that is gained through enlightenment is asparsha yoga, which can be understood as discovering the 'relation-less I' of paramArtha. Relationships have their place in vyavahAra but can never bring about self-knowledge. (Ref. 34)

459 People may well feel good during the satsang, reinforcing an idea that it is 'working' but as soon as they get back to their everyday life, all is as it was before. 'Feeling good' is not, and will not bring about, enlightenment.

It is, nevertheless, true to say that someone with severe psychological problems may well have difficulty hearing/appreciating/ accepting the teaching, since those psychological issues will cloud the mind. Accordingly, it is certainly desirable to resolve them first. ('Everyday' psychological problems will naturally be resolved through exposure to traditional teaching.)

460 There is also the danger of transference. Many satsang teachers specifically discourage practice of any kind, reading scriptures, meditation etc. and neo-advaitins in particular will openly state that bhakti yoga of any kind is futile. And yet nothing is usually said to dissuade seekers from effectively worshiping the teacher. Traditional teachers will have practiced chatuShTaya sampatti, one result of which is the development of natural humility. They would only allow a student to 'worship' them if this was positively helpful to the student and in this case the teacher would treat it as directed to the sampradAya and not to him or herself personally.

461 Many seekers are only trying to relieve mental stress, and find peace in their lives through the acquisition of temporary moments of happiness. They do not appreciate that enlightenment is not simply another experience. Seekers tend to find teachers who will satisfy their particular needs. In this scenario, the notion of enlightenment will indeed become a mere 'story' because this sort of seeker and this sort of teacher will never bring it about.

462 In such a situation, both (inauthentic) teacher and (inauthentic) student may be satisfied. The teacher receives adoration and the seeker is told that 'this is it, now; there is nothing that needs to be

done' etc. Superficially, it is a 'win-win' situation but, as far as spiritual truth is concerned, it is actually a 'lose-lose' one.

463 Most seekers seem to judge the 'success' of a satsang and therefore the efficacy of the teacher, not by the loss of self-ignorance but by the gaining of a spurious 'detachment' and temporary loss of the sense of a separate ego or even simply a feeling of euphoria.

'Experiences' and 'states' have nothing to do with Self-realization. Philip Mistlberger points out: "It is common to confuse the ego in a state of no anxiety with an authentic spiritual realization." (Ref. 24)

464 Neo advaitins claim that whatever is the case in the 'story' of the seeker, whether it be confusion, identification or suffering, that *is* reality and, by definition, is 'ok'.

As usual, this is to confuse paramArtha and vyavahAra and, from the vantage point of the deluded jIva, it is no help at all.

Morality

465 The neo-advaitin view that 'there are no others' and 'there is no free will anyway' may also be interpreted as a license to act in whatever way one desires, regardless of the wishes of others. Whatever arises must be the 'desire' of the Absolute, since I am already That and there is nothing else.

This is a dangerous position. The introduction of ideas such as these from a respected authority at a time of personal vulnerability could outweigh current conditioning and bring about 'out of character' actions that might hurt others, whose separate existence remains a fact in vyavahAra. Traditional advaita states that the person has limited free will. dharma (effectively morality in this context) should always underpin the aims of artha (wealth and security) and kAma (desire for pleasurable things and experiences) in our lives. [dharma, artha, kAma and mokSha are held by traditional teachings to be the four primary aims of life.] Furthermore, traditional teaching does not accept that brahman can have desires, since this would contradict the essential pointer of 'unlimited'. As the Katha Upanishad (I.2.24) states: "The Self cannot be known by anyone who desists not from unrighteous ways, controls not his senses, stills not his mind, and practices not meditation." *(Ref. 99)*

466 Some teachers use the metaphor of the cinema screen – films of fire and flood are shown but the screen is totally unaffected – to argue that anything may happen but it doesn't really matter because no one is actually impacted. This is the usual confusion again. The nondual brahman is unaffected but people are very much affected.

The traditional attitude is clearly expressed in the Bhagavad Gita (III.21 – 26). The enlightened man has a responsibility always to set a standard for others by his actions. Although, being enlightened, he has nothing further to achieve, he nevertheless continues to act, but without attachment, for the benefit and guidance of humanity. "A wise person will not disturb the mind of an unwise person who is still attached to the fruits of his or her actions. But by continuously performing perfect (selfless) actions the wise person influences others in all they do." (Ref. 77)

467 The ultimate truth of advaita (that the duality of the world is only apparent, depending for its reality upon the non-dual brahman) does not alter the appearance and cannot be used to excuse behavior. In vyavahAra, there are people who act and they may do so in a way which is morally good, bad or indifferent. The fact is that there is evil and suffering in the world and it remains the responsibility of the student of advaita to recognize this and behave accordingly – even more so, if he or she should be enlightened. Many people, even those who have attended satsangs for a long time may not appreciate this.

468 Andrew Cohen coined the phrase 'advaita shuffle' for the way in which an unscrupulous teacher sometimes twists the tenets of advaita for their own ends. *"...any difficulty that one is faced with... can be 'Advaited' by saying that it is all unreal or all the Self anyway... However, this confidence becomes a form of arrogance, a form of self-delusion, when it is used to avoid one's own difficulties..."* (Ref. 78)

469 Absolute reality is untouched by any action which I perform; any action which takes place in the world of seeming duality. However in the world where actions do take place, where the seeker lives out his life, if he 'does what he wants' and breaks the law for example, he will end up in prison or worse. He is most *unlikely* to end up 'enlightened'!

470 Similarly, many teachers state that it makes no difference whether we carry out any kind of spiritual practice. The conclusion is that, if we are practicing, we might as well give up.

Alan Jacobs says that: "The injunction to give up spiritual practice is dangerous, as it allows the vAsanA-s full permission to indulge, and leads to a dead-end of hedonism, or at best a parking space until the next 'satsang fix'. There is no grace without effort. One either wants an illusory but comfortable self-calming quietness, or one wants enlightenment." (Ref. 38)

471 A traditional teacher acknowledges a responsibility towards his disciples and would only communicate ego-destroying ideas if on-hand subsequently to monitor the fallout and help resolve the problems. It is simply not possible for most Western satsang teachers to do this. (They effectively plant the bombs and then flee the scene!)

In fact, traditional teachers are not really interested in 'destroying egos'. The aim is to differentiate between satyam and mithyA. Methods such as those already described naturally lead the seeker to cease to identify with the ego without the need for any specific 'attack'.

472   There is also the danger of 'misbehavior' on the part of the teacher whenever that teacher has not experienced the rigorous preparation of a traditional background. Being virtually worshipped by many young and attractive seekers presents frequent temptation. And the position of authority enables the teacher to change attitudes towards morality as well as spirituality.

For many other problems associated with teachers who ought not to be teaching, see Ref. 53.

Characteristics of seeker

473   In the West, satsang is now the favored form of teaching, while traditional-style study with a guru for 'as long as it takes' is very much frowned upon. Most seekers would probably drop out of a traditional class very quickly – it is too much like being back at school! The fact that this attitude mirrors the Western values of individualism and instant gratification might in itself cause one to ask searching questions concerning the popularity of the 'satsang' phenomena.

474   There are very few, formal guru-disciple relationships with Western teachers. Most are very casual. Teachers travel round the world giving satsangs, stopping off for a weekend in a major city and seekers often switch allegiance to whoever happens to be in their vicinity or according to which one is currently fashionable.

475   Most seekers don't want to have to do anything to become enlightened... and this is exactly what neo-advaitin teachers tell them is the case. The devotional practices of bhakti yoga or the

'right actions' of karma yoga have little appeal to the Western mind.

As James Swartz puts it: "But most of the people who attend these neo-advaita satsangs have not done sAdhanA, don't know what it is, and wouldn't do it anyway. In general they are looking for instant enlightenment." (Ref. 55)

476 But one does also find, amongst the satsang attendees, many seekers who *have* carried out traditional practices, possibly for many years, but have become disillusioned, feeling that they are not progressing. The 'nothing to do' concept obviously appeals to these, too. One will invariably find, however, that these seekers were not being guided by a qualified teacher and their 'lack of progress' can be attributed to this. The practices alone may prepare the mind but it is self-knowledge alone that brings enlightenment.

477 The untutored seeker does not know what questions to ask to understand the nature of reality. This is why a prolonged course of teaching is required first.

478 Because many attendees are 'casual', there may not be genuine commitment, with more interest in the meeting aspect than in listening to the teacher, and in the seeking of a spiritual experience rather than a gaining of self-knowledge. In traditional teaching, seekers are prepared, focused and committed to a prolonged program with the clear goal of enlightenment.

479 It is necessary to address seekers at their present level of understanding. Often, neither the student nor the teacher appreciates this. The seeker wants to feel that they are ready for the most advanced teaching and may think they are being patronized if more basic material is presented first. And a weak teacher may be afraid of addressing what are considered to be 'obvious' points (Latin – ob via, meaning 'in the way'), lest the student feels that the teacher is

inept, has missed the point or is attacking them.

480 Unless seekers are spiritually advanced, they are unable to understand the 'higher' teachings. As an analogy, someone wishing to understand quantum mechanics will not immediately appreciate an advanced text on the subject – they must first learn about mathematics and basic physics.

*Initially the world is believed to be real and separate. Traditionally, the first stage of teaching is that the world is not **in itself** real (c.f. the rope-snake and dream metaphors). Only much later is it revealed that mithyA is, in the final analysis, also satyam. This practice is the same in Buddhism with its 'mountains are initially seen as mountains, then later seen as not mountains and finally seen again as mountains' (but now known to be only a form of the non-dual reality). In traditional advaita, everything is 'neti, neti' before it is eventually realized that 'sarvaM khalvidaM brahmA' (all this is verily brahman).*

481 Consequently, if the seeker is not 'ready' (i.e. qualified – see 340), he will be unable to perform shravaNa, manana and nididhyAsana adequately and the teaching will not have the desired effect.

Characteristics of teacher

482 There is an implicit assumption that satsangs are what is implied by the word, i.e. 'association with the wise'. Seekers assume that the teacher is both enlightened and qualified to teach. The two do not necessarily go together. Ideally, a teacher will be enlightened but, if he or she is also to be a good teacher, there must be in-depth knowledge of effective teaching methodologies and many skills, including compassion and the ability to empathize with the seeker.

483 Even if the teachers are enlightened, there is no guarantee that they will be able to help with the removal of the self-ignorance in others.

Swami Satprakashananda points out that: *"Even a knower of nirguNa brahman, unless he is thoroughly acquainted with the arguments for and against the Vedic teachings, cannot dispel all doubts and misconceptions of the seeker."* (Ref. 17) [nirguNa means 'beyond the guNa-s, i.e. the unmanifest, attribute-less brahman.]

484   Most satsang teachers have themselves spent some time with one or more teachers but few can claim any real connection with a sampradAya. Even fewer have undergone any formal tuition in traditional methods. Most have little familiarity with the scriptures and scarcely any know Sanskrit (though these are not absolutely essential).

485   Books of their satsangs are published and sell well to new seekers, who believe that what is being said is authentic. In fact, the more radical a teacher is (i.e. the more distant from the traditional), the more this appeals to publishers and readers with the result that much that passes as advaita in the West bears little relation to it.

486   Many modern satsang teachers may claim to have had only one or two 'experiences' of non-duality and think that this qualifies them to teach.

As noted earlier, enlightenment has nothing to do with 'experiences', which come and go. It is to do with constant abidance in the knowledge of the non-dual nature of all appearances.

487   A teacher will only ever be able to teach up to their own level of understanding. This has two consequences. Firstly, the students will complete their 'course', possibly knowing as much as the teacher and consequently thinking that they are now enlightened. Secondly, from the point of view of the teacher, since the student now knows as much as they do, the student must also be qualified to teach. This explains how it comes about that teachers who themselves have

dubious qualifications are nevertheless authorizing students to begin teaching.

488 It follows that many teachers are liable not only to have insufficient knowledge but may also lack the capability to communicate what they do know.

489 Many satsang teachers (and all neo-advaita teachers) attempt to teach only the ultimate reality. They make few concessions to the present condition of the seeker.

It is no use telling the 'truth' at the beginning (even assuming this were possible ultimately), since our preconceptions, opinions and past experience would simply reject it. Neo-advaita attempts to do this, which is one of the reasons why it fails as a teaching method. It does not recognize the process of sublation or the technique of adhyAropa-apavAda.

490 Many satsang teachers and all neo-advaitin teachers imply that the non-dual truth is somehow self-evident, that there is nothing new to be discovered to make this fact apparent.

In fact, the only self-evident truth is that 'I am'. The facts that I am unlimited (ananta), that 'there is only That' and that 'I am That' are not initially self-evident. There is thus a need for the scriptures (to provide the methodology) and a guru who knows how to use them.

491 Satsang teachers, especially neo-advaitins, rarely if ever utilize recognized techniques or prakriyA-s. This may be because they themselves are unfamiliar with such techniques. Instead of proven teaching methods, most of their material depends upon unverifiable claims, using undefined terminology, about the nature of reality. The language of such claims can readily be acquired by attending other satsangs. Consequently, it is difficult to authenticate the status

of these teachers.

Gilles Farcet, in Ref. 53, compares this situation with someone about to undergo an operation. Just as we would naturally check out the credentials of the surgeon before entrusting our body to the knife, we also ought to check out the teacher to whom we are entrusting our spirit, as it were. But we rarely do.

492 Traditional (sampradAya) teachers invariably hold their own teacher in reverence and constantly acknowledge the lineage as the authority, effectively an unbroken line back to the truth. (In this sense, they continue to be disciples themselves.) Satsang teachers, especially those who claim independence from any lineage or specific teacher, consider *themselves* as the (effectively sole) authority.

493 As already noted, the literal meaning of satsang is association with the good or wise. When a teacher is part of a sampradAya, that is valuable and reliable evidence for supposing that he or she is indeed good and wise. When a teacher is self-proclaimed, their probity and wisdom are always going to be questionable.

494 Because most of them lack the grounding of Vedantic knowledge, they depend upon intuition and personal experience for answering questions. This is not always adequate.

495 Therefore, there is significant danger of charlatans who are difficult to expose because true 'teaching' as such is virtually non-existent in the West. Good actors can easily delude the seeker, especially when these to some degree actually want to be deluded. This is even more certain to happen when the teachers are themselves deluded!

496 Satsang teachers are usually clever, witty, attractive etc. – this is a large part of their appeal. But none of these are relevant to the tradi-

tional teacher – what is important is their ability to teach.

497 Satsang teachers are quite likely to enjoy their fame and notoriety, travelling to more and more places to spread their message. Traditional teachers rarely travel - seekers go to them; they have no interest in whether or not they have disciples and shun fame and fortune.

498 Traditional teachers never ask for money - seekers usually go to the teacher at their own cost. If they do travel to teach, their hosts usually pay their expenses. Satsang teachers almost invariably do ask for money and pay their own costs out of the proceeds, presumably usually leaving a healthy income.

499 The attitude of the true teacher is expressed by Nisargadatta Maharaj (although he, too, was effectively giving satsang to those who visited him): *"You come and listen to me and go. If you want it, take it. If not, go away. The space in this room is neither for, nor against, nor in love with, the space in that room; it is one. Like a river flowing, if you want to utilize it, you take the water and drink it, assimilate it; otherwise, let it flow past. I am not charging you, just like the river is not charging you for the water. You are spending a lot of money every day; come on, you put your money away and take my water."* (Ref. 12)

500 Some satsang teachers encourage the idea that enlightenment can be transmitted from guru to disciple (i.e. by simply being in their presence). This fits in with the 'nothing to do' idea and also makes people keep coming back in the hope that the effect might be cumulative… like radiation.

501 Such ideas having nothing to do with advaita and, in Ref. 2, I called such teaching 'pseudo-advaita' to differentiate it from more legitimate forms. Timothy Conway comments: *"Thinking of Self-*

realization as a 'transmission' from one personality to another hooks people into what can be called the 'Grace chase.' It is a tricky way for someone to 'inflate' or overvalue his or her own role in the process of sharing wisdom and then feel justified in charging money (or worse) for his/her services. Many who presume to be teachers 'transmitting' Self-realization, set up in their listeners the idea or expectation of 'getting something,' and getting it from 'me.' This is a classic 'salesman' trick—create a need and then an expectation, and then have the audacity to suggest that 'I will fulfill your need and expectation.'"

502 Many of the retreats of satsang teachers are 'silent' retreats. This seems to stem from the idea that some past sages used to teach through silence. But the word actually used in the scripture in reference to the sage dakShiNAmUrti is mudrA, meaning 'a sign made by the position of the fingers' and should be interpreted as 'language'. Cynically, it is obviously a very easy source of income to have students pay to attend meetings at which one doesn't even have to speak! From the point of view of the seeker, although such a retreat is likely to be a peaceful experience, it is most unlikely that any self-ignorance will be dispelled.

Neo-advaitin Teaching

503 Neo-advaitin teachers who have not themselves received prior tradi-tional-style teaching are frequently unable to give satisfactory answers to seekers. Often, if a student's observation from experience contradicts what has been said by the teacher, the latter simply states that it is all 'paradoxical'.

It is also quite possible that they simply do not know the answer. It is not usual for any such teachers to admit this, since to do so would undermine their authority. Accordingly, there may be a temptation to use sarcasm or some other linguistic tool to put an end to the question (and decrease the likelihood of further questions from that source).

504 Neo-advaitin teachers often make use of the paradoxes entailed in the paramArtha-vyavahAra distinction to attempt to ridicule traditional teaching. It is nevertheless a necessary distinction if we are to speak meaningfully about both our present experience in the world and about the non-dual reality.

*Failure to recognize this results in just as many paradoxes and illogicalities on the part of the teacher, beginning with the fact that he or she **is** teaching.*

505 A common 'mantra' of neo-advaitin teachers in particular is 'this is it'. It seems to be expected that this will be enough to bring about enlightenment – it isn't. 'This is it' is helpful to the extent that it is impersonal and thus egoless. It is also a modern restatement of such Upanishadic statements as *sarvam khalvidam brahma (all this is verily brahman)*. But the ego-sense of the seeker usually continues unabated. What such statements do not tell the seeker is *tat tvam asi* (you are That).

Neo-advaitin teachers do not acknowledge this because they claim that 'you' are a non-existent entity, a 'story', and so on.

506 Having condemned the use of Sanskrit words, which in traditional teachings have very specific meanings, many satsang teachers and especially neo-advaitin ones make up their own language. These newly-coined words, or novel ways of combining existing words, only assume an imagined meaning through frequent usage. If analyzed logically, what they say is often meaningless. Words should always make sense, both on their own, and in the context in which they are used. If they do not, ask the speaker for clarification or, if reading a book, discard it.

507 In recognition of the fact that in reality there are no separate persons, many satsang teachers have developed a mode of expression that enables the speaker to make clear to listeners that this fact is understood. They do this by speaking in the passive sense, i.e. instead of saying 'I did this', they say 'it was done' and so on.

Traditional teachers know that the 'I thought' is the fundamental experience at the empirical level of reality so have no problem with speaking naturally. This artificial way of speaking has come to be known as the 'Lucknow' syndrome in honor of the location in India where Sri Poonja used to hold his meetings.

508 Neo-advaitin teachers have gone one stage further in recent years in not simply recognizing but positively emphasizing that there are no persons. No longer is it sufficient to say 'it was seen' instead of 'I saw'; now neo-advaitins say 'it was seen by no one'.

509 Neo-advaita has a single answer for all, even when (as is very often the case) the student does not have sufficient background understanding to be able to appreciate that answer.

510 The very claims of neo-advaita - that there is no seeker, no teacher and nothing to be taught - invalidate it as a teaching method.

Everything is already perfect, say the neo-advaitins - there is not really anything further that needs to be said. Whether the illusory person is 'enlightened' or not makes no difference - it is all just part of the story.

511 This is true, of course, at the level of ultimate reality. There is only brahman, which is perfect and complete (pUrNam) and that is that – *end* of story! But this is clearly not the end of the story in the phenomenal realm because neo-advaitin teachers continue to hold

regular satsangs and publish books of their 'dialogs'. And, more importantly, seekers remain enmeshed in their self-ignorance.

512 One has to ask: why do these teachers teach? If there is 'no teacher, no seeker, no path etc', what are they doing? Surely it is not simply a cynical way of earning a living?

513 Neo-advaitin teachers have often themselves spent many years seeking, despite the fact that they state that this is pointless.

514 Neo-advaita attempts to give you the final truth from the outset and this is in keeping with the modern Western ethos of wanting everything now. We don't want partial truths or to be patronized with merely a glimpse of the whole picture. Unfortunately it is almost invariably the case that this "final truth" does not help.

515 Crucially, if the seeker accepts the ideas that they are already free, that there is no seeker, nothing to be done, nothing that *can* be done etc, they are forever locked into their situation with no way out other than the random grace that might just occur through continuing indefinitely to attend more satsangs. Any sense of responsibility is taken away from the seeker as well as any belief that they can or need to change their situation.
See 300 and 315 for clarification.

516 The messages that 'this is all there is' and 'this is already perfect' are contradictory statements for the typical seeker, who is usually suffering and looking for something better. The message is confounding the attitude of the seeker with that of the enlightened person, another variant of the paramArtha-vyavahAra confusion. The presence of the ignorance makes one see the snake in the rope even though the snake doesn't actually exist. The fear that results is all too real in its effect.

517 In the worst cases, the claimed futility of further seeking can lead to a total sense of hopelessness on the part of the seeker. Unfortunately, many teachers in such a situation rarely seem to have any sympathy or empathy and can offer no help other than to reiterate that there is no one in need of any help.

518 Since satsang teaching of any kind is unable to provide any support to seekers once they have left the meeting, the 'world-shattering' conclusions of neo-advaita ought to be approached very circum-spectly.

519 It also has to be said that the minimalist message of neo-advaita with its formulaic mantras can easily be learnt by the unscrupulous, or unintentionally absorbed by an uncritical mind. Any voluble and quick-witted individual could then offer themselves as a teacher, whether truly enlightened, honestly deluded or merely cynical.

Timothy Conway comments: "The truth is that 'giving satsang' in the way many people do it today is the easiest thing in the world. Once one has learned some of the Absolute-truth rap (easily available after reading just a few books or articles), a certain basic peacefulness and ease in social settings, and, last but not least, the dialectical questioning 'maneuvers' (e.g., 'Who is asking the question?' 'Who wants enlightenment?' 'Have you traced that thought/feeling back to its source?' 'What would you be if you gave up that belief?' etc. etc.) one could 'give satsang' easily, endlessly, while half-asleep. It all flows out quite 'effortlessly' from the condi-tioning one sets up in the mind." (Ref. 80)

520 In the extreme, satsangs and books by such teachers may simply consist of repetition of what are essentially meaningless phrases, which only have the superficial appearance of actually saying something profound. Behind such hollow pronouncements, it is perfectly possibly that there lies no true understanding at all.

Is the teacher enlightened?

521 One of the most significant aspects regarding any teacher who is not part of a sampradAya (to formally authorize them) is the question of their enlightenment. In all of the preceding discussion, the 'benefit of the doubt' has been given and the assumption made that all teachers, traditional or otherwise, are enlightened. But this claim has to be considered in connection with what is meant by the term. An earlier section listed all of the erroneous definitions that are made by various sources (not necessarily teachers of advaita it must be said). The following section gave various correct statements according to traditional advaita. It follows that, if a particular teacher's definition of enlightenment is invalid (according to traditional advaita), any claim to their actually being enlightened must be in doubt.

522 Neo-advaitin teachers even deny that there is such a thing as enlightenment. Jeff Foster: *"There is, of course, no such thing as enlightenment, there is no 'ultimate' state, no way to meditate one's way to Nirvana, no way to 'get rid' of the ego."* (Ref. 75)

523 Traditional teachers do not often make claims regarding their own enlightenment and are reluctant to discuss the status of other teachers. They are teachers in the purest sense, unfolding the knowledge of the scriptures, with humility, for the benefit of the student; there is simply no interest in receiving adulation of any kind. However If pressed, and if it is useful for the student to know in order to explain or illustrate a particular point, there is no problem with affirming self-knowledge.

524 The intrinsic format of the Western-style satsang, on the other hand, assumes that the teacher is fundamentally different from the student and, even if not actively encouraged, reverence of the teacher as a 'superior being' is implicitly sanctioned. This, in turn, emphasizes the feeling that the seeker almost certainly already has, of being

inferior and inadequate.

525 It has been pointed out by a reviewer that those who claim to have been enlightened as a result of attending satsangs often begin an aggressive self-promotion campaign via a book or website, offering satsangs in their own right. Such publicity and hype might seem somewhat incongruous in the context of non-duality.

526 The differences between the enlightened teacher and the non-enlightened usually only becomes apparent through prolonged association with them. Fundamentally, the unenlightened are forever seeking satisfaction from the mithyA world. They perceive themselves to be lacking and wish to satisfy that lack by fulfilling their desires (and losing their fears). Their happiness is dependent upon these temporary successes and they retain a feeling of inadequacy. The enlightened still have desires but are no longer dependent upon their fulfillment in any way – they know that they are already full and complete. Specifically, then, there is no 'disappointment' when wishes or expectations are not met, nor 'elation' when they are.

527 There is no easy or fast method for determining whether a given teacher is enlightened. Satsang teachers often speak or write of their 'enlightenment experience', even if this is given a different name such as 'seeing through the story'. Most of the attendees will take what is said as true and accept that the teacher *is* enlightened, even if no agreed definition has been reached. This is a grave mistake.

Such enlightenment 'stories' are also likely to mislead the seeker into thinking that some dramatic experience needs to occur at some time in the future, rather than the simple, incremental gaining of direct knowledge vRRitti-s in the present.

528 Since neo-advaitin teachers deny the existence of the person,

ignorance and enlightenment, they are patently unenlightened according to their own definition.

529 The concern must be that many satsang teachers do not really know what enlightenment is and are consequently mistaken about their own status. They may thus be unqualified to be giving satsang to seekers, in which case seekers will be most unlikely to benefit. Indeed, by taking in erroneous concepts and being pointed in what is often quite the wrong direction, they may gain more ignorance rather than lose that which they already have.

530 Why do seekers pay money to attend talks by someone who uses no proven method or documented system and who effectively admits that he or she is not enlightened? Why would they think that such teachers are qualified to hold satsangs? There are three possible answers:

 a) it is assumed that the teacher IS enlightened (even if this only amounts to the final understanding that there is no such thing as enlightenment);

b) it is the appeal of a 'path' that entails zero effort on the part of the seeker – they can have enlightenment NOW without having to do anything at all;

c) they are simply following the crowd, assuming that their peers cannot all be wrong and not wanting to be left out. Whichever is the case, such a seeker is suffering self-delusion.

What Should You Do?

What should you do if you are a seeker?

531 The most important, and ultimately most effective, action that could be taken is to find a traditional teacher who will accept you as a disciple. Second best is to find a school based upon traditional teaching and guided by a realized sage, who is frequently physically accessible to all students.

NB. There are dangers with a school. If most of the teachers are themselves still students, it is likely that they will be neither Self-realized nor shrotriya-s. They may not even be very good at explaining what they do know. Though not necessarily an obstacle in the early stages, this can become a serious problem later on. Accordingly, it is important that all students have access to a fully qualified teacher and that senior students are taught directly by one.

532 A 'threefold-verification' is sometimes spoken of to assist in this: Does the teaching match that given in the scriptures? Does it match the teaching of a known Sage? Is what is spoken of verifiable in one's own experience?

533 In the absence of a teacher or school, as an interim measure, read the scriptures and writings of modern sages.

Rather than reading from just one or two sources, it is probably better to read many different sources, without regarding any one as 'absolute'. It is important to remember that it is not possible to speak directly of the truth, only 'point' in the right direction. Also, one must endeavor not to interpret new concepts in old ways. Ideally, the mind would be emptied first, to avoid the problem explained by the Zen metaphor of trying to pour tea into a cup which is already full. If the style of a particular writer does not resonate, look for another.

534 Discuss the subject, especially areas of confusion, with like-minded and more mature seekers. A particularly useful opportunity for this is on the serious Egroups on the Internet (e.g. the advaitin group at Yahoo).

535 If you must attend satsangs, do so with extreme caution (having read this book!).

536 Do not accept the essentially unverifiable pronouncements of neo-advaita regarding your existence as a 'story' and the meaning-lessness of paths and teachers.

Ask the following question of your neo-teacher: "Why should I believe you rather than the evidence of my own senses and reason? Why should I reject the proven teachings of the past thousand years in favor of what you are saying?"

What should you do if you are a satsang teacher?

537 Answer yourself honestly – Are you really enlightened, according to the traditional concepts of the term? If not, go to 531. There need be no problem with this since even someone who is self-realized may wish to learn traditional techniques in order that he may teach effectively in later life. (Of course, if you fear the loss of face that would accompany an open admission, this is confirmation that there is still an ego!)

538 You should stop travelling around the world and instead offer long courses in your own locality, providing you are able to utilize proven teaching methods.

These should probably be at least 1-year duration (at the rate of, say, 3 hours per week) for beginners and perhaps shorter for long-term seekers. But you should present clear topics and not simply answer questions.

539 Ideally, you should 'unfold' the scriptures, interpreting the sometimes difficult passages for modern ears.

Unfortunately, it is unlikely that anyone who has not been formally taught to do this would be able to.

Summary of main points

540 We are ignorant of our true nature and that of the world. As a result of self-ignorance we believe that we are a separate body-mind, subject to the vicissitudes of an alien world. We feel, or have been led to believe, that there might be a 'way out of this' through becoming 'enlightened'. We therefore seek self-knowledge from a teacher who, we believe, is able to provide this.

541 The effect of self-knowledge is to remove the ignorance that prevents the realization that we are already brahman. To the extent that the mind was prepared through sAdhana chatuShTaya sampatti, there is also the secondary, emotional benefits (jIvanmukta) such as contentment, love, fearlessness etc.

542 In the traditional teachings the process of obtaining this knowledge is gradual, holistic, and undifferentiated by all the distinctions used by satsang and neo-teachings – there is no single 'can-opener' that might enable everyone instantly to attain to this final self-knowledge. And it is not indirect - you're never in the wrong place or being taught ignorance.

543 There are immediate, direct knowledge 'vRRitti-s' in response to hearing the words of the teacher. The knowledge is immediate because it is about our own self and requires no other external reference.

544 We may be said to be 'enlightened' when the self-knowledge is complete, namely when, knowing that one is the Self, one is also established in j~nAna niShThA - the full and final knowledge that this Self is all that there is.

545 Traditional teaching has long-established, logical procedures (prakriyA-s) for using the scriptures as a means of knowledge

(pramANa). Explanations appropriate to our current understanding are presented. As we progress, those explanations are supplanted by more sophisticated ones.

546 The scriptures function to inform us of the fact that the Self (Atman) is brahman; that I am unlimited existence-consciousness. These are not self-evident facts. Experience only tells us that 'I am'.

547 Neo-advaita attempts to speak directly of the non-dual reality. This is impossible, since language, teacher and seeker are all at the level of the dependent, dualistic world. Since all of the seekers' prior understanding concerns vyavahAra and they hold a firm belief in their existence as separate, suffering individuals, such teaching is unlikely to be helpful. 'Explanations' frequently mix up the levels and cause further confusion.

548 Traditional teaching has many gauged methods so that the skilled teacher may present whichever is most suited to the student's level of understanding. The satsang method is forced to be 'one size for all' since it is a stand-alone event with no continuity.

549 All seeking, suffering, teaching, practice and enlightenment take place in vyavahAra, where the 'person' has a modicum of free will and where effect follows cause according to natural law. It is brahman, at the absolute paramArtha level, who is 'already liberated' etc.

550 Appropriately guided effort and the direct assimilation of knowledge, as revealed by the pramANa, will most likely result in enlightenment; 'doing nothing' will achieve nothing. That guidance must come from someone who understands our problems irrespective of the fact that they will ultimately be discovered not to have been real problems at all.

551 The neo-advaitins' denial of the world means that they can never help the seeker in any way, since they deny the existence of such an entity. In fact, they have a net negative effect since they often turn the seeker away from a path that might have led somewhere, leaving them lost in a forest of misunderstanding. They can also encourage lack of concern for the suffering of others and even immoral behavior.

552 Traditionally, the mind of the seeker must be prepared to receive self-knowledge. Otherwise, we may hear the truth but simply not be able to make sense of it or assimilate it. Neo-advaita claims that all practice is irrelevant since there is no person, no 'doing' or free will, no ignorance, no path and no enlightenment. In fact, all of these *always* appear to exist and are only realized not to exist in reality after enlightenment.

553 Furthermore, if the traditional preparations (sAdhana chatuShTaya sampatti) are not undergone, although we may become enlightened, we will not reap the secondary benefits of a steady and peaceful mind.

554 Modern Western satsang teaching consists of occasional question and answer sessions given to whomsoever turns up, regardless of their level of understanding, by teachers who rarely have any real connection with formal sampradAya methods. Questions will be random and answers unlikely to be relevant to all.

555 A teacher should ideally be enlightened, a shrotriya and be able to utilize the traditional methods. (It goes without saying that they should also be a skillful teacher in the usual sense.) Satsang teachers rarely belong to a sampradAya and probably have neither read the scriptures nor have familiarity with their techniques. Accordingly their wisdom, teaching ability and probity are always liable to be suspect. Unfortunately, there is no way for the seeker to determine

whether a teacher is enlightened.

556 The minimalist message of the neo-advaitin lends itself to misuse by those who wish to exploit the gullible.

557 Seekers should reconcile themselves to the fact that a path to enlightenment is a significant and possibly long-term undertaking. Ideally, they should find a traditional teacher who will take responsibility for their tuition. Failing that, an organization guided by such a teacher is likely to be the best option.

558 As an interim measure, reading and discussion can be very valuable but attending satsang meetings cannot really be recommended, given the problems and dangers that have been outlined in this book.

559 Satsang and neo-advaitin teachers should consider learning traditional methods and then simply teaching groups of students for extended periods (in the teacher's home town).

Conclusion

Over the past 30 – 40 years, there has been an accelerating trend in the West towards the use of the satsang as the sole method for teaching Advaita. This probably stems from the popularity of the transcriptions of talks by Ramana Maharshi and Nisargadatta Maharaj but gained momentum when many new teachers claimed the blessing of Sri Poonja. Traditionally, a sampradAya teacher would only authorize disciples as teachers in their own right when he had been able to confirm their enlightened status and verify their complete understanding of the teaching methods of the scriptures. Today, scarcely any satsang teacher in the West can claim this authority.

Neo-advaita is a relatively recent development. In this, the traditional teaching has been impoverished to the point of extinction with nothing remaining of its wealth of methods and its ability to cater for all levels and types of seeker. Instead, all that remains is a Gaudapada-like statement of the nature of absolute reality – something that is meaningful only to the most advanced student. Since most of the seekers attending these meetings are not advanced, their confusion and suffering is exacerbated rather than relieved.

Increasingly, it seems that other satsang teachers are also moving in this direction. This may well be the natural result of the format of the satsang being ill-suited to genuine teaching. Since seekers attend only occasional meetings, often with different teachers and usually with different students, there is no continuity and the message needs to be conveyed in a short time. Western society also wants (and expects) instant results. Questions are typically from the vantage point of the person looking to satisfy egotistical desires relating to happiness, relationships etc. and are frequently irrelevant to other students.

The fundamental problem is the self-ignorance in the mind of the seeker as a result of adhyAsa. Appropriate knowledge is needed and this has to be acceptable to the mind, which must be able to exercise reason and discrimination, not be confounded by past opinions and beliefs and so on. All of this takes place naturally as part of the teaching process under the guidance of a skilled teacher. Therefore, at the level of the world, there are seekers who do things. Ideally, they should prepare the mind through appropriate practices and follow a formal, proven, logical path to gain self-knowledge, with the help of a competent guide. Only on successful completion will they fully realize that they always have been brahman. All of this is in direct contradiction to the teaching of neo-advaita.

Where there is darkness, light is needed. Traditional teaching provides that light in the form of gradual, structured, tailored and reasoned explanation that can be verified in our own experience and must lead ultimately to realization of the truth. Neo-advaita attempts to bypass all of this and present the final conclusion without any arguments. Lacking the logic, it also proves ineffectual. The less absolutist satsang teaching may attempt to utilize some of the methodology of traditional teaching but, lacking the structure, context and continuity, it too is doomed to failure in the majority of cases.

Most satsang teachers also appear to stress the negative aspects – neti, neti; not the body, mind, ego etc. - and their end-point is that what is left is who you really are. The fact is, though, that the nature of this 'what is left' is not usually explained. The result is that seekers are given a relatively nihilistic view of reality. In the case of neo-advaita, this combines with the view that, since there is no one to do anything and the world is an illusion anyway, then whatever we might do makes no difference. Thus, for some people, an amoral outlook might be considered a logical result of hearing such teachings.

This is entirely opposite to the traditional approach, in which pointers to who we are (brahman) are given. The mahAvAkya 'tat tvam asi' dismantles our erroneous concepts about 'thou' but at the same time emphasizes that we are 'That' so there is never any question of a void or emptiness. On the contrary, who we are is full and complete (pUrNa) and limitless (ananta).

Many of these modern teachers attempt to argue that their teaching is appropriate to the time, that the scriptures are no longer relevant and that our educated and sophisticated minds can accept the final truths now without the traditional circuitousness and indirection. In fact, our present-day self-ignorance is the same as it has always been. We still identify with body, mind and roles and still believe that there is a real world of separate objects and other people. It is these fundamental issues that are addressed by traditional methods – what we are not and what we are. The sampradAya-s have proven techniques for resolving these issues. Simply stating the conclusions, as neo-advaitin teachers do, will never be effective since those conclusions are quite contrary to our apparent experience.

Because most modern teachers lack the formal, traditional background of authenticity; because of the casual format of satsang and the attenuated teaching content, it is becoming increasingly easy for anyone to set themselves up as a teacher without actually having any credentials – and there is no 'college of licensed advaitin teachers' which we can check.

Seekers and teachers alike need to reconcile themselves to the fact that there can be no short-term measures. We have generations of wrong thinking to rectify so that we may learn to look at ourselves and the world in a completely different way that contradicts our present beliefs. Instinct, habit and deeply-held opinion can never be overturned by a brief question and answer session on no particular topic by individuals, each with their own agenda. It requires a prolonged, coordinated inquiry, using proven techniques, with the help of teachers skilled in using those techniques. Genuine seekers of the truth must find a teaching environment that satisfies these requirements and the onus is on today's Western satsang teachers to provide it.

Acknowledgements

I wish to offer my sincere thanks to the following, who read various early drafts of the book and provided comments. Some of these comments were incorporated verbatim but the associated reviewers preferred that their quotes not be attributed.

Mariana Caplan, Timothy Conway, Greg Goode, Katherine Hellen, Alan Jacobs, Edward Kowaloff, John Lehmann, Kathy Lehmann, Philip Mistlberger, Allan Nineberg, Anne Nuss, Chris Quilkey, James Swartz, William Wharton.

Definition of Key Terms

AchArya – spiritual guide or teacher.

adhikArI – a seeker who is mentally prepared (see chatuShTaya sampatti) and therefore ready to receive the final teaching from the guru; literally "possessing authority, entitled to, fit for." adhikAra effectively means 'eligibility'.

adhyAropa apavAda - the teaching technique whereby an attribute is applied to brahman initially but is later taken back, once the point has been understood (since brahman cannot actually have attributes). adhyAropa means 'erroneously attributing one thing to another' and apavAda means 'denial or contradiction.' An example would be the teaching of the kosha-s or five 'sheaths' which are suggested 'cover up' our true nature.

adhyAsa - used to refer to the "mistake" that we make when we erroneously "superimpose" a false appearance upon the reality or mix up the real and the unreal. The classical example is when we see a snake instead of a rope, which is used as a metaphor for seeing the world of objects instead of the reality of the Self. This concept is fundamental to advaita and Shankara devotes a separate section to it at the beginning of his commentary on the Brahmasutra.

advaita - the non-dual philosophy, based upon the Upanishads and systematized by Shankara around the 8th Century AD.

AgAmin - That type of saMskAra which is generated in reaction to current situations and which will not bear fruit until sometime in the future. It literally means "impending," "approaching" or "coming." Also called kriyamANa, which means "being done."

ahaMkAra - the making, kAra, of the utterance "I," aham – this is the equivalent of what we would call the "ego" but specifically refers to the identification or attachment of our true Self with something else, usually the body or mind but can be much more specific e.g. I am a teacher, I am a woman. It is one of the "organs" of the mind in classical advaita.

akhaNDAkAra vRRitti - the mental 'occurrence' which effectively causes enlightenment. This is the vRRitti (thought) in the form of

(AkAra) the formless or undivided (akhaNDa).

ananta - eternal, without end, unlimited.

antaHkaraNa - used to refer to the overall "organ" of mind; the seat of thought and feeling.

anugraha - grace; literally showing favor or kindness, conferring benefits; used at the level of the world, in connection with belief in a divine being who 'brings us' knowledge, a teacher and ultimately enlightenment.

aparokSha – immediate (of knowledge).

Ashraya – locus.

Atman - the Self. Usually used to refer to one's true (individual) nature or consciousness but advaita tells us that there is no such thing as an 'individual' and that this Atman is the same as the universal Consciousness, brahman.

AvaraNa - the veiling power of mAyA. In the rope-snake metaphor, this power prevents us from seeing the reality of the rope.

avidyA - ignorance (in a spiritual sense) i.e. that which prevents us from realizing the Self.

bAdha – sublation - this is the process by which an accepted point of view or understanding is superseded by a totally different one when some new information is received. An example is seeing a lake in the desert and then realizing that it is only a mirage.

bhAga tyAga lakShaNa - a technique used by the scriptures to point to aspects that cannot be explained directly in words. The oneness that is pointed to (lakShaNa) is understood by "giving up" (tyAga) the contradictory parts (bhAga). An example would be in the apparent contradiction of the jIva being "created" while Ishvara is the "creator." Both are given up in order to recognize their identity as brahman.

bhakti yoga - devotion or worship as a means to enlightenment.

bhAmatI – literally "lustrous"; name of one of the two schools of Advaita, also called the vAcaspati school, after the philosopher vAcaspati mishra. The other school is the vivaraNa school.

brahman - the universal reality, Self, Absolute, God or Godhead.

brahmaniShTha – literally, one who 'stands in brahman'; more generally, one who is enlightened.

buddhi - the organ of mind responsible for discrimination and judgment, perhaps nearest equated to the intellect in Western usage.

chatuShTaya sampatti – the fourfold pre-requisites specified by Shankara as needed by a seeker before he can achieve Self-realization.

dama – self-restraint but understood as control over the senses; one of the six qualities that form part of Shankara's chatuShTaya sampatti.

dehAtma buddhi – the belief that I am this body-mind.

dRRigdRRishya viveka - "Discrimination between the Seer and the Seen" – a work attributed to Shankara. dRRik is the seer or perceiver and dRRishya that which is seen or which can be objectified.

enlightenment - (Note that this term will be defined differently by different teachers and neo-advaita denies its existence.) It is self-ignorance that prevents recognition of the truth about our nature and that of reality. Enlightenment takes place in the mind of a person when all of that ignorance has been eradicated. (Note that all of this is only meaningful at the empirical level of existence, which is why the statements of the neo-advaitins are not absolutely false.)

guNa - According to classical advaita, creation is made up of three "qualities," sattva, rajas and tamas.

guru - literally "heavy"; used to refer to one's elders or a person of reverence but more commonly to indicate one's spiritual teacher. (It is also sometimes said to mean 'disperser of darkness' on the grounds that gu and ru stand for darkness and light respectively.)

haTha yoga – (a later name for) the physical aspects (Asana and prANayAma) of rAja or aShTA~Nga yoga (the method devised by Patanjali).

jIva - the identification (by ahaMkAra) of the Atman with a body and mind; sometimes spoken of as "the embodied Atman."

jIvanmukti – the emotional benefits of Self-knowledge; the 'secondary' gain of enlightenment. A jIvanmukta is one is both enlightened and who lives with these benefits, which manifest in outward love and compassion.

j~nAna yoga - yoga based on the acquisition of true knowledge (j~nAna means "knowledge") i.e. knowledge of the Self as opposed to mere information about the world of appearances. See vidyA.

j~nAnI or j~nAnin - one who practices j~nAna yoga, but more often used in the sense of a 'realized man', i.e. one who knows the truth.

j~nAna niShThA – the full and final knowledge that this Self is all that there is.

kArikA - (strictly speaking) a concise philosophical statement in verse. The most well known is that by Gaudapada on the Mandukya Upanishad. (Not to be confused with karika, which is an elephant!).

karma - literally "action" but generally used to refer to the "law" whereby actions carried out now will have their lawful effects in the future (and this may be in future lives).

karma yoga - the practice of acting in such a way as not to incur karma, by carrying out "right" actions, not "good" or "bad" ones.

kartRRi-tantra – the result of 'doing' (activity, desire and effort), as opposed to vastu-tantra, begotten of Atma).

kuNDalinI - a type of yoga, supposed to awaken the power (kuNDalin is a 'snake') at the base of the spine and cause it to rise up through the chakra-s to the brain. This is nothing to do with advaita.

lakShaNa - pointer; indicating or expressing indirectly; accurate description or definition.

manana - the clearing of doubts by asking questions on what has been heard (shravaNa) from the guru. This is the second stage of the classical spiritual path.

mAyA - literally "magic" or "witchcraft," often personified in Hindu mythology. The "force" used to explain how it is that we come to be deceived into believing that there is a creation with separate objects and living creatures etc.

mithyA - dependent reality; literally "incorrectly" or "improperly," used in the sense of "false, untrue." It is, however, more frequently used in the sense of "depending upon something else for its existence." It is ascribed to objects etc., meaning that these are not altogether unreal but not strictly real either i.e. they are our imposition of name and form upon the undifferentiated Self.

mokSha - liberation, release from saMsAra.

mudrA - particular positions or ways of intertwining the fingers, commonly practiced in religious worship.

mumukShutva - the desire to achieve enlightenment, to the exclusion of all other desires.

neo-advaita - the style of teaching that purports to express only the final, absolute truth of advaita. It does not admit of any 'levels' of reality and does not recognize the existence of a seeker, teacher, ignorance, spiritual path etc.

neti, neti - not this (na – not; iti – this). From the bRRihadAraNyaka Upanishad (2.3.6). Used by the intellect whenever it is thought that the Self might be some "thing" observed e.g. body, mind etc.

nididhyAsana - meditating on what has been directly seen at the time of teaching until it is known as a fact (immediate experience, not requiring intellectual reasoning). The third stage of the classical spiritual path.

nirguNa - "without qualities"; usually referring to brahman and meaning that it is beyond any description or thought. Since there is only brahman, any word would imply limitation or duality.

nyAya prasthAna - refers to logical and inferential material based upon the Vedas, of which the most well known is the brahmasUtra of vyAsa.

pa~ncha kosha prakriyA – the traditional teaching that the Self is, as it were, covered over by five 'sheaths' like a dagger. These are food (i.e. the body), vital air, mind, intellect and bliss.

paramArtha (noun), pAramArthika (adj.) - the highest truth or reality; the subjective noumenal as opposed to the phenomenal world of objective appearances (vyavahAra).

paramparA - literally "proceeding from one to another"; "guru paramparA" refers to the tradition of guru – disciple passing on wisdom through the ages.

phala – fruit; used in the metaphorical sense of a resultant gain, usually in respect of karma (action), where the result is either puNya (merit) or pApa (misfortune). It is also used in respect of the emotional benefits of self-knowledge – j~nAna phala or jIvanmukta.

prakriyA - a methodology of teaching; literally a chapter (esp. the introductory chapter of a work).

pramANa - valid means for acquiring knowledge. There are traditionally 6 of these (fully explained in Ref. 2):

a) *Direct perception – pratyakSha.* This includes the external senses – sight, hearing, touch, taste and smell – for perceiving so-called objects and the internal, mental perception of feelings or awareness of knowledge and so on.

b) *Inference – anumAna.* There cannot be any inference unless there is some prior knowledge gained from direct perception.

c) *Comparison or analogy – upamAna.* This effectively says the following: If A (which is directly perceived now) is similar to B (which is something perceived before and now remembered), then B is also similar to A.

d) *Non-apprehension – anupalabdhi.* This states that not perceiving something is the same as perceiving that thing's non-existence.

e) *Postulation or supposition – arthApatti.* This is the situation where we can directly observe something that is not explainable unless we assume something else to be the case. The classic example that is used is observing that someone whom we know does not eat during the day is nevertheless getting fat. We assume that he must be eating during the night when we are not watching.

f) *Verbal authority or evidence – shabda.* In the case of all of the above, our own direct perception is involved in one way or another. In the case of shabda, we rely on the testimony of others.

prArabdha - This literally means "begun" or "undertaken." It is the fruit of all of our past action that is now having its effect. This is one of the three types of saMskAra.

prANa - literally the "breath of life"; the vital force in the body with which we identify in the "vital sheath."

prasthAna traya - the three sources of knowledge of the Self, nyAya prasthAna, shruti and smRRiti.

pUrNa - full, complete, satisfied, perfect.

rajas - the second of the three guNa-s, associated with animals and activity, emotions, desire, selfishness and passion.

sAdhaka - a seeker or, more pedantically, a worshipper.

sAdhanA - literally "leading straight to a goal"; refers to the spiritual disciplines followed as part of a "path" toward Self-realization.

samitpANi - (literally) holding fuel in the hands, i.e. having renounced all desire and approaching the deity to offer sacrifice.

sampradAya - the tradition or established doctrine of teaching from master to pupil through the ages.

saMnyAsin - one who has undertaken saMnyAsa, the final stage of the traditional Hindu spiritual path; involves complete renunciation.

saMsAra - the continual cycle of death and rebirth, transmigration etc. to which we are supposedly subject in the phenomenal world until we become enlightened and escape.

saMskAra - Whenever an action is performed with the desire for a specific result (whether for oneself or another), saMskAra is created for that person. These accumulate and determine the situations with which we will be presented in the future and will influence the scope of future actions. There are three "types" – AgAmin, saMchita and prArabdha. The accumulation of saMskAra (saMchita) dictates the tendencies that we have to act in a particular way (vAsanA-s). This is all part of the mechanism of karma.

sarvaM khalvidaM brahmA – all this (universe) is verily brahman (from the Chandogya Upanishad (III.14.i).

satsang (satsa~Nga) – (In the context of this book) the style of teaching popular in the West, whereby the teacher hosts short meetings of an hour or two or longer 'residential' courses of up to one or two weeks. The teacher may speak on a topic for a short time but, more usually, attendees ask whatever question might be on their mind and the teacher endeavors to answer this. Note that, in its traditional use, the word literally means 'association with the wise or good'. It refers to a meeting in which some teaching is given, followed by question and answer. This is essentially the same meaning; the difference is that it forms just a part of traditional teaching whereas it is the entirety of most Western teaching.

sattva - the highest of the three guNa-s, associated with stillness, peace, refinement, harmony, truth, wisdom, unselfishness and spirituality.

satyam – truth; the 'truly real' as opposed to the 'dependently real' mithyA.

shabda - scriptural or verbal testimony.

shama – self-control; one of the shamAdi ShaTka sampatti or "six qualities" that form part of Shankara's chatuShTaya sampatti.

shiShya - pupil, scholar, disciple.

shravaNa - listening to the teachings (of such works as the Upanishads) unfolded by the guru; first of the three key stages in the classical spiritual path.

shrotriya - someone who is well-versed in the scriptures.

shruti - refers to the Vedas, incorporating the Upanishads. Literally means "hearing" and refers to the belief that the books contain orally transmitted, sacred wisdom from the dawn of time.

siddhi - supernatural power which may supposedly be acquired by advanced seekers (but of no interest to the serious seeker).

smRRiti - refers to material "remembered" and subsequently written down. In practice, it refers to books of law (in the sense of guidance for living) which were written and based upon the knowledge in the Vedas, i.e. the so-called dharma-shAstra-s. In the context of prasthAna traya, it is usually used to refer to just one of these books – the Bhagavad Gita.

sublation (bAdha) - This is the process by which an accepted point of view or understanding is superseded by a totally different one when some new information is received or a new perspective is reached. An example is seeing a lake in the desert and then realizing that it is only a mirage. (Note: This is also sometimes written 'subration'.)

tamas - the "lowest" of the three guNa-s, associated with matter and carrying characteristics such as inertia, laziness, heedlessness and death.

tattvamasi - one of the four 'great sayings' (mahAvAkya-s), meaning 'thou art That'.

trikAlAtIta - that which transcends past, present and future (describing reality or the Self).

tuchCha – empty, vain, trifling, little; also used in the sense of 'totally unreal', c.f. prAtibhAsika.

turIya - literally the "fourth" [state of consciousness]. It refers to the non-dual reality, the background against which the other states (waking, dream and deep sleep) arise. It is our true nature.

upAdhi - Literally, this means something that is put in place of another thing; a substitute, phantom or disguise. In Vedanta, it is commonly referred to as a "limitation" or "limiting adjunct" i.e. one of the "identifications" made by ahaMkAra that prevents us from realizing the Self.

vastu-tantra – objective, governed by reality (as opposed to kartRRi-tantra or puruSha-tantra, the result of 'doing').

vichAra - consideration, reflection, deliberation, investigation or inquiry. vichAra mArga is translated as "Direct Path."

vidyA - knowledge in the sense of science, learning, scholarship and philosophy (or, in a more derogatory sense, 'information). See j~nAna.

vikShepa - the "projecting" power of mAyA. In the rope-snake metaphor, this superimposes the image of the snake upon the rope.

vivaraNa - literally "explanation" or "interpretation"; name of one of the two schools of Advaita. The other school is the vAchaspati or bhAmatI school.

vRRitti - a mental disposition.

vyavahAra (noun), vyAvahArika (adj.) - the relative, practical, or phenomenal world of objective appearances; the normal world in which we live and which we usually believe to be real; as opposed to pAramArthika (reality) and prAtibhAsika (illusory).

Bibliography

1   The Book of One, Dennis Waite, O Books, 2003, ISBN
    1903816416.

2   Back to the Truth, Dennis Waite, O Books, 2007, ISBN
    1905047614.

3   Being: the bottom line, Nathan Gill, Non-Duality Press, 2006.
    ISBN 978-0-9551762-2-7.

4   Already Awake, Nathan Gill, Non-Duality Press, 2004. ISBN 0-
    9547792-2-3.

5   Notes on Spiritual Discourses of Shri Atmananda taken by Nitya
    Tripta, 2nd Issue not yet published. Electronically available from
    http://www.advaita.org.uk/.

6   Extracts from 'Tony Parsons in Amsterdam: Saturday 27th July
    2002', Tony Parsons, downloaded from his website at
    http://www.theopensecret.com/index.shtml.

7   Perfect Brilliant Stillness, David Carse, Non-Duality Press, 2005,
    ISBN 0954779282.

8   Four Quartets, T. S. Eliot, Faber and Faber Limited, 1979, ISBN
    0-571-04994-X.

9   Private Email communication, Nathan Gill, Feb 2006. Reproduced
    in Ref. 2.

10 Spiritual Enlightenment - The Damnedest Thing, Jed McKenna,
    Wisefool Press, 2002, ISBN 0-9714352-3-5.

11   Both=One, John Greven, essay at advaita.org.uk
      (http://www.advaita.org.uk/discourses/trad_neo/both_one_greven.h
      tm), Oct 2005.

12   Prior to Consciousness: Talks with Sri Nisargadatta Maharaj,
      Edited by Jean Dunn, The Acorn Press, 1985. ISBN 0-89386-024-
      7.

13   Be Who You Are, Jean Klein, Non-Duality Press, 2006, ISBN 978-
      0-9551762-5-8.

14   Atmabodha (Knowledge of Self), A. Parthasarathy, Vedanta Life
      Institute, 1971, No ISBN.

15   From Self to Self, Leo Hartong, Non-Duality Press, 2005, ISBN 0-
      9547792-7-4.

16   (Awakening to) The Natural State, John Wheeler, Non-Duality
      Press, 2004, ISBN 0-9547792-3-1.

17   Methods of Knowledge according to Advaita Vedanta, Swami
      Satprakashananda, Advaita Ashrama, 1965. ISBN 81-7505-065-9.

18   Life After Death: A Former Racing Driver's Story Of Spiritual
      Awakening, Charlie Hayes, BookSurge Publishing, 2006, ISBN
      097661985.

19   Living Reality: My Extraordinary Summer with 'Sailor' Bob
      Adamson, James Braha, Hermetician Press, 2006, ISBN 0935895-
      10-8.

20   Seeds for the Soul, Chuck Hillig, Trafford Publishing, 2003, ISBN
      1-55395-844-6.

21   The Teachers of One: Living Advaita - Conversations on the
      Nature of Non-duality, Paula Marvelly, Watkins Publishing, 2002,
      ISBN 1 84293 028 1.

22   The Truth Is, Sri H. W. L. Poonja, Yudhishtara, 1995. No ISBN.

23   Post to the Advaitin Egroup, July 2006, V. Subrahmanian.

24   A Natural Awakening: Realizing the True Self in Everyday Life, P.
      T. Mistlberger, TigerFyre Publishing, 2005. ISBN 0-9733419-0-4.

25   Post to the SatsangDiary Egroup, Tanya Davis, Sept. 2006.

26   Brahma Sutras, Swami Sivananda, The Divine Life Society.
      Electronically available from
      http://www.swami-krishnananda.org/bs_00.html.

27   The Method of the Vedanta: A Critical Account of the Advaita
      Tradition, Swami Satchidanandendra Translated by A. J. Alston,
      originally published by Kegan Paul International, 1989. ISBN 0-
      7103-0277-0, edition now listed and distributed by Shanti Sadan,
      www.shantisadan.org.

28   Talks with Sri Ramana Maharshi, Sri Ramanashramam, Recorded
      by Sri Munagala Venkataramiah, 1955. No ISBN. (Available for
      free download at http://www.ramana-maharshi.org/.

29   I Hope You Die Soon: words on non-duality, Richard Sylvester,
      Non-Duality Press, 2006, ISBN 978-0-9551762-1-0.

30   Dialogues with Swami Dayananda, Sri Gangadhareswar Trust,
      1988. No ISBN.

31   Maha Yoga or The Upanishadic Lore in the Light of the Teachings

of Bhagavan Sri Ramana, "Who", Sri Ramanasramam, 1937. No ISBN. Electronically available from http://www.ramana-maharshi.org/.

32   The Wisdom of Balsekar, Edited by Alan Jacobs, Watkins Publishing, 2004. ISBN 1 84293 079 6.

33   Right Here, Right Now: Seeing Your True Nature as Present Awareness, John Wheeler, Non-Duality Press, 2006. ISBN 978-0-9551762-3-4.

34   Classes on mANDUkya upaniShad and kArikA-s, H.H. Swami Paramarthananda, mp3 CDs or audiotapes available from http://www.sastraprakasika.org/.

35   Introduction to Vedanta, Dr. K. Sadananda, Advaitin Egroup Jan. 2007.

36   The Open Secret, Tony Parsons, The Connections, 1995. ISBN 0 9533932 0 9.

37   Seeing and Not Seeing, Tony Parsons, Article in Self Enquiry, Feb 2004, (Bi-Annual Review of the Ramana Maharshi Foundation UK.) ISSN 1357 0935.

38   Western Advaita Teachers - An Overview, Alan Jacobs, Article in Self Enquiry, Feb 2004, (Bi-Annual Review of the Ramana Maharshi Foundation UK.) ISSN 1357 0935.

39   Psychological Advaita, Atreya Smith, Article in Self Enquiry, Dec 02/January 2003, (Bi-Annual Review of the Ramana Maharshi Foundation UK.) ISSN 1357 0935.

40   Day by Day With Bhagavan, A. Devararaja Mudaliar, Sri

Ramanasramam, 2002. ISBN 8188018821. Electronically available from http://www.ramana-maharshi.org/.

41   The Teaching of the Bhagavad Gita, Swami Dayananda, Vision Books Pvt., 1989. ISBN 81-7094-032-X.

42   Four Quartets, T. S. Eliot, Faber and Faber Limited, 1979. ISBN 0-571-04994-X.

43   The Adhikara: To Form a Vessel, Vamadeva Shastri (David Frawley), Article in Self Enquiry, August 2000, (Tri-Annual Review of the Ramana Maharshi Foundation UK.) ISSN 1357 0935.

44   Nothing Personal: Seeing Beyond the Illusion of a Separate Self, Nirmala, Endless Satsang Press, 2001. No ISBN. Electronically Available from http://www.enlightenedbeings.com/nirmala.html.

45   Awake Living Joy: The Essence of Spiritual Enlightenment, Katie Davis, Unpublished Manuscript, 2004.

46   Acceptance of What IS – A Book About Nothing, Wayne Liquorman, Advaita Press, 2000. ISBN 0-929448-19-7.

47   Tony Parsons, Amigo Oct. 2002. Electronically Available from http://www.ods.nl/am1gos.

48   I am, Jean Klein, compiled and edited by Emma Edwards, Non-Duality Press, 2006 . ISBN 978-0-9551762-7-2.

49   vivekachUDAmaNi – Talks on 108 Selected Verses, Swami Dayananda Saraswati, Sri Gangadharesvar Trust, 1997. No ISBN.

50   The question to life's answers: Spirituality Beyond Belief, Steven

Harrison, Sentient Publications, 2002. ISBN 0-9710786-0-2.

51   A primer on Advaita, Francis Lucille. Electronically Available
       from http://www.francislucille.com/.

52   A Collection - Talks and Essays of Swami Dayananda, Sri
       Gangadhareswar Trust, 1999. No ISBN.

53   Halfway up the Mountain: The Error of Premature Claims to
       Enlightenment, Mariana Caplan, Hohm Press, 2001. ISBN 0-
       934252-91-2.

54   Zen: Dawn in the West, Roshi Philip Kapleau, Vintage/Ebury,
       1987. ISBN 0-091406-11-0.

55   Email from James Swartz. Electronically Available from
       http://www.shiningworld.com/Satsang%20Pages/HTML%20
       Satsangs%20by%20Topic/Neo-Advaita/Teaching%20enlight-
       enment.htm

56   Do You Need a Guru?, Mariana Caplan, Thorsons, 2002. ISBN 0
       00 711865 1.

57   Be As You Are: The Teachings of Sri Ramana Maharshi, Edited by
       David Godman, Arkana, 1985. ISBN 0-14-019062-7.

58   In the Jungle, Robert Adams, Self Enquiry (Tri-annual Review of
       the Ramana Maharshi Foundation, U.K.), Vol. 8 No. 2, Aug. 2000.
       ISSN 1357-0935.

59   The Supreme Yoga: yoga vAsiShTha, Swami Venkatesananda,
       Chiltern Yoga Trust, 1981. ISBN 81-208-1964-0.

60   Mandukya Upanishad, Swami Chinmayananda, Central Chinmaya

Mission Trust, 1990. No ISBN.

61   The mANDUkya upaniShad, with gauDapAda's kArikA and
      shaMkara's commentary, translated by Swami Nikhilananda,
      Advaita Ashrama, 1987. No ISBN.

62   dRRigdRRishya viveka - An Inquiry into the Nature of the 'Seer'
      and the 'Seen', translation and commentary by Swami
      Nikhilananda, Sri Ramakrishna Ashrama, Mysore, 1976. ISBN
      090247927X.

63   Dialogues on Reality: An Exploration into the Nature of Our
      Ultimate Identity, Robert Powell, Blue Dove Press, 1996. ISBN 1-
      884997-16-3.

64   You Are That! Satsang With Gangaji, Volume 1, Gangaji, The
      Gangaji Foundation, Jan. 1995. ISBN 096321943X. Extracts
      electronically available at http://www.gangaji.org/.

65   How to Meet Yourself... and find true happiness, Dennis Waite, O
      Books, 2007. ISBN 1-84694-041-9.

66   The Outrageous Myths of Enlightenment, Stephen Wingate, Atma
      Publishing, 2006, ISBN 0-9787254-0-9.

67   Post to the SatsangDiary Egroup, Tanya Davis, Nov. 2004.

68   Being, Conversations with Florian Tathagata, Thomson Press,
      2006. ISBN 1-905479-01-8.

69   The Daydream Unmasked: Interview with Jan Kersschot, 2005.
      Electronically available from
      http://www.kersschot.com/nobodyhome/index.
      php/interview_2005.

70   Choice Upanishads, A. Parthasarathy, 2001. No ISBN.

71   Personal email discussion with a student of Swami Dayananda, April 2007.

72   An Edited Transcript of an Interview with Richard Sylvester, 29th Oct. 2005. Electronically available from http://www.richardsylvester.com/index.php?pr=Interview.

73   Where Are We Going? The Fate and Failings of Contemporary Spirituality, Mariana Caplan, ReVision Magazine, Spring, 2001. Electronically available from http://www.realspirituality.com/articles.html.

74   Kena Upanishad (Rediscovering Indian Literary Classics, no. 3), Translation and Commentary by Swami Muni Narayana Prasad, D. K. Printworld (P) Ltd., 1995. ISBN 81-246-0034-1.

75   Life Without a Centre: Awakening from the Dream of Separation, Jeff Foster, Non-Duality Press, 2006. ISBN 0-9553999-0-4.

76   Private Email communication (in review of this book), Greg Goode, Apr 2007.

77   The Living Gita (The Complete Bhagavad Gita), A commentary for modern readers, Sri Swami Satchidananda, Integral Yoga Publications, 1988. ISBN 0-932040-27-6.

78   The Advaita Shuffle, Part 1: The Perils of the 'Advaita Shuffle' or These Days Is the Absolute View Used As an Excuse to Avoid Waking Up Fully?, B.R., What Is Enlightenment? 1, no.1 (Jan 1992): 12, quoted in Ref. 53.

79   Tricks of the Tirade, Sarlo's Guru Rating Service. Electronically
      Available from http://www.globalserve.net/~sarlo/Shtick.htm.

80   Neo-Advaita or Pseudo-Advaita and Real Advaita-Nonduality:
      Traps and Pitfalls in the "Neo-Advaita" or "Pseudo-Advaita" form
      of Advaita (Nondual) Spirituality, Timothy Conway. Electronically
      available from http://www.enlightened-spirituality.org/neo-
      advaita.html.

81   upadesha sAhasrI of shrI shaMkarachArya, translated into English
      with explanatory notes by Swami Jagadananda, Sri Ramakrishna
      Math, 1989. ISBN 81-7120-059-1.

82   Four Upanishads, Swami Paramananda, Sri Ramakrishna Math,
      1974. ISBN 81-7120-233-0.

83   The Twelve Upanishads Vol. 3, Raja Rajendralal Mitra & E. B.
      Cowell, D. K. Printworld (P) Ltd., 1906. ISBN 81-246-0166-6.

84   A Tradition of Teachers: Shankara and the Jagadgurus Today,
      William Cenkner, Motilal Banarsidass, 1983. ISBN 81-208-1763-x.

85   Discourse on KenopaniShad, Swami Chinmayananda, Central
      Chinmaya Mission Trust, 1952. No ISBN.

86   Eight Upanishads with the commentary of Shankaracharya, Vol.1,
      Translated by Swami Gambhirananda, Advaita Ashrama, 1957.
      ISBN 81-7505-0160-0.

87   The Bhagavad Gita with the commentary of Sri Sankaracharya,
      Alladi Mahadeva Sastry, Samata Books, 1977. No ISBN.

88   Brahma Sutra Bhashya of Shnakaracharya, Translated by Swami
      Gambhirananda, Advaita Ashrama, 1996. ISBN 81-7505-105-1.

89   Vakya Vritti, Adi Sankaracharya, Translated by Swami
       Chinmayananda, Chinmaya Mission, Electronically Available at
       http://www.sankaracharya.org/vakyavritti.php.

90   The Ten Principal Upanishads, Put into English by Shree Purohit
       Swami and W. B. Yeats, Faber and Faber, 1937. ISBN 0 571
       09363 9.

91   Shankara on Enlightenment (A Shankara Source Book Volume 6),
       compiled and translated by A. J. Alston, Shanti Sadan, 2004.
       ISBN 0-85424-060-8.

92   The Mandukyopanishad With Gaudapada's Karikas And The
       Bhashya of Sankara, translated into English by Manilal N.
       Dvivedi, Tookaram Tatya, F.T.S, 1894, reprinted by Kessinger
       Publishing. ISBN 1428643060.

93   Ten Upanishads of Four Vedas, Researched and Edited by Ram K.
       Piparaiya, Bharatiya Vidya Bhavan, 2003. ISBN 81-7276-298-4.

94   The Principal Upanishads, S. Radhakrishnan, HarperCollins
       Publishers India, 1994. ISBN 81-7223-124-5.

95   Kathopanishad, Swami Chinmayananda, Central Chinmaya
       Mission Trust, 1994. No ISBN.

96   Mandukya Karika of Gaudapada, translated by Vidyavachaspati V.
       Panoli, Electronically Available from
       http://www.geocities.com/advaitavedant/mandukyakarika.htm.

97   The Geeta: The Gospel of the Lord Shri Krishna, put into English by
       Shri Purohit Swami, Faber and Faber, 1935. ISBN 0 571 06157 5.

98   Katha Upanishad, translated by Vidyavachaspati V. Panoli,

Electronically Available from
http://www.celextel.org/ebooks/upanishads/katha_upanishad.htm.

99   The Upanishads, Translated and with a general introduction by
      Eknath Easwaran, Penguin Books 1994, Copyright Juan Mascaró
      1965. ISBN 0-14-019180-1.

100   Discourse on Mundakopanishad, Swami Chinmayananda, Central
      Chinmaya Mission Trust, 1988. No ISBN.

101   Locus of Ignorance, Post to Advaitin Egroup, S. N. Sastri, Aug.
      2007.

Index

Note: References are to paragraph numbers, not page numbers. References in **bold** relate to principal entries.

AvaraNa, **48**, 76
avidyA, 46, 86, 200, 274

B

bAdarAyaNa, 43, 117
bAdha, 81
Balsekar, Ramesh, 243, 362
becoming, end of, 276
beliefs, 146
bhAga tyAga lakShaNa, 38, **426**
Bhagavad Gita, 246, 291, 315,
    376, 466
bhakti yoga, 321, 407
bhAmatI school, 47, 70, 72
blind leading blind metaphor, 394,
    395
blindfolded in forest metaphor,
    385
bliss, 230
blue sky (apparent attribute), 44
blue sky metaphor, 123
books
    of satsangs, 485
    reading, 355
brahma sUtra, 42, 116
brahma sUtra bhAshya, 47
brahman, 21, **22**, 42, 43, 52, 78,
    79, 106, 109, 117, 169, 170,
    201, 224, 264, 265, 266, 271,
    546
    does not act, 202
    does not become enlightened,
    262
    knowing that I am, 61

locus of ignorance, 47
    not a doer, 296
    not an object, 425
    we must already be, 312
brahmaniShTha, 63, **131**
brahmasatyam etc., 179
Brasso metaphor for
    enlightenment, 90
breathing, 254
Brihadaranyaka Upanishad, 47,
    376
buddhi, 286
Buddhism, 480
butter in milk metaphor, 283

C

Capricorn One, 40
Carse, David, 337, 394
casual attendees, 478
catapult metaphor for
    enlightenment, 95
causality, 202, 251, 305
    effects have causes, 304
    none, 303
    operates at level of world, 343
Cenkner, William, 399
center of attention, 444
certainty, 279
chakra-s, 258
Chandogya Upanishad, 385
change, subject to, 276
channelling, 215
characteristics of seeker, **473–81**
characteristics of teacher, **482–502**

Krishna Menon, Atmananda, 112,
152
kuNDalinI yoga, 258

L

lakShaNa-s, 425
language, 6, 77, **169**, 502
as pointers, 338
meaningless, **506**, 520
part of vyavahAra, 192
level of seeker, 451
level of understanding, 479
levels of consciousness, 243
levels, confusion of, **195**, 225,
296, 314, 319, 343, 464, 516,
547
liberation, 86
from notion that we are bound,
295
idea of, 365
light, 236
light and darkness metaphor, 323
light in dark room metaphor, 92
likes and dislikes, 205
limiting adjunct, 292
Linden, Roger, 273
lineage, 150
logic, 138, 155
Lucknow syndrome, 507

M

macrocosmic, 201
magic eye paintings metaphor,
268

mahAvAkya-s, 64, 426
as pramANa, 119
manana, **66–74**, 481
Mandukya Upanishad, 79, 125,
173, 191, 197, 214, 274, 414
Mars, film of mission, 40
materialism, 269
maTha-s, 139
mAyA, **198–201**, 364
McKenna, Jed, 396, 442
meaning, 2, 228
versus experience, 327
meaning of life, 117
meeting size, 443
mental preparation, 82, 117, 284,
348, 349, 364, **406–11**, 552
merging with Self, 213
mesmerization, 187, 317
metaphor
blind leading blind, 394, 395
blindfolded in forest, 385
butter in milk, 283
chocolate vs $100 bill, 351
cinema screen, 466
clay pot, 113, 190
clouds and sun, 366
diseased wood, 328
dream, 325
drink from river, 499
faces vase, 273
fire and wood, 368
fog lifting, 91
friend and film star, 426
going to school, 414

can be chosen, 297
cannot be chosen, 296
none, **333–38**
purpose of, 323
significant undertaking, 557
perception, 29, 33, 39
periods of enlightenment, 220
person, **105–9**, 170, 360
appearance of name and form,
266
belief in, 83
belief that I am separate, 264
enlightened, 272
I am not, 109
no person, only a story, 293
none to become enlightened,
108
not an illusion, 369
paradox need not be a problem,
311
point of view, 272
seeing through the illusion, 369
that is enlightened, 53, **222**,
263
Philosophy Foundation, 138
pointers, positive, 425
Polaroid photograph metaphor, 91
pole vault metaphor, 415
Poonja, Sri, 148, 435, 507
popular does not mean good, 396
positive aspect of teaching, 75
positive pointers, 425
postulation, 29
pot space metaphor, 104, 213

practice, **283**, 331, 398, 470
belief that enlightenment is in
future, 346
does not reinforce ego, 367
fire and wood metaphor, 368
needed for enlightenment, 340
of no value, **339–70**
purpose of, 323
relates to mental preparation,
365
takes us away from under-
standing, 345
prakriyA-s, 402, **419–31**, 491, 545
pramA, 28
pramANa-s, 28, **29**, 54, 545
prArabdha karma, 227, 250
prasthAna traya, **116**, 140
pratibhAsa, **113**, 174
Pratima, 435
pratyakSha, 29
premonitions, 253
preparation of the mind. *See*
mental preparation
present, being, 86
probity, 493
progress, 476
monitoring, 377
to enlightenment, 94
projecting power, 48
protons etc., 189
pseudo advaita, 501
psychic powers, 252
psychology of satsangs, **457–64**
publicity, 525

BOOKS

O books

O is a symbol of the world, of oneness and unity. In
different cultures it also means the "eye", symbolizing
knowledge and insight, and in Old English it means "place
of love or home". O books explores the many paths of
understanding which different traditions have developed
down the ages, particularly those today that express
respect for the planet and all of life.

For more information on the full list of over 300 titles
please visit our website
www.O-books.net

SOME RECENT O BOOKS

Back to the Truth
5000 years of Advaita
Dennis Waite

This is an extraordinary book. The scope represents a real tour de force in marshalling and laying out an encyclopaedic amount of material in way that will appeal both to the seasoned and to the introductory reader. This book will surely be the definitive work of reference for many years to come.
Network Review

1905047614 600pp **£24.95 $49.95**

Everyday Buddha
Lawrence Ellyard

Whether you already have a copy of the Dhammapada or not, I recommend you get this. If you are new to Buddhism this is a great place to start. The whole feel of the book is lovely, the layout of the verses is clear and the simple illustrations are very beautiful, catching a feel for the original work. His Holiness the Dalai Lama's foreword is particularly beautiful, worth the purchase price alone. Lawrence's introduction is clear and simple and sets the context for what follows without getting bogged down in information... I congradulate all involved in this project and have put the book on my recommended list.
Nova Magazine

1905047304 144pp **£9.99 $19.95**

Everything is a Blessing
David Vennells

I've read a few self-help books in my time, but this is the only one I've ever talked about with no reserve or irony. Vennells charmed me utterly with his open enthusiasm, simple presentations of deep spiritual truths, suggestions for achievable goals and workable plans and doable exercises. It leaves readers with the feeling of having been spoken to directly by someone who genuinely cares about them and wants to help them heal and succeed.
Marion Allen fiction site

1905047223 160pp **£11.99 $19.95**

Mysticism and Science
A Call for Reconciliation
Swami Abhayananda

A lucid and inspiring contribution to the great philosophical task of our age – the marriage of the perennial gnosis with modern science.
Timothy Freke author of *The Jesus Mysteries*

184694032X 144pp **£9.99 $19.95**

One Self
Philip Jacobs

Philip Jacobs has explained the almost inexplicable idea of "Oneness" probably as clearly and accessibly as is possible here, and without religious bias. Recognising the need for a metaphorical approach to illuminate this esoteric concept, he is liberal with his use of helpful parables and anecdotes from many sources, ancient and modern. He explores topics such as consciousness, identity, suffering, happiness, love, freedom and meaning,

and I particularly liked the chapter on illness. He has provided an all round summary for anyone new to, or renewing a path of spiritual growth.
Pilgrims

1905047673 160pp **£9.99 $19.95**

Ordinary Women, Extraordinary Wisdom
The Feminine Face of Awakening
Rita Marie Robinson

This will become a milestone in female spirituality. Not only does it recount the fascinating and intimate stories of twelve 'ordinary' women in their search for peace and self knowledge, the author engages the reader with her own quest through her integrity, vulnerability and courage. Beautifully written with captivating honesty, this unique book will become an inspiration for both men and women alike, also looking for the essence of who they truly are.
Paula Marvelly, author of *Teachers of One*

9781846940682 256pp **£11.99 $24.95**

Practicing Conscious Living and Dying
Stories of the Eternal Continuum of Consciousness
Annamaria Hemingway

This is a glorious book. A science of immortality is in the making, and Annamaria Hemingway is one of its architects.
Larry Dossey, MD, author of *The Extraordinary Healing Power of Ordinary Things*

9781846940774 224pp **£11.99 $24.95**

Science of Oneness
Malcolm Hollick

A comprehensive and multi-faceted guide to the emerging world view. Malcolm Hollick brilliantly guides the reader intellectually and intuitively through the varied terrains of the sciences, psychology, philosophy and religion and builds up a vibrant picture that amounts to a new vision of reality for the 21st century. A veritable tour de force.
David Lorimer, Programme Director, Scientific and Medical Network

1905047711 464pp **£14.99 $29.95**

Suicide Dictionary
The History of Rainbow Abbey
Paul Lonely

This is a startlingly original work of sheer genius – highly recommended, if you can handle it.
Ken Wilber, author of *The Integral Vision*

9781846940613 176pp **£7.99 $16.95**

Supreme Self
Swami Abhayananda

"The Supreme Self" is a very authentic book by a very authentic man. It is not only a personal testament on the importance of pursuing your highest spiritual path with absolute dedication and intent, but it is also a wonderful synopsis of mystical religions and their numinous goals. Swami

Abhayananda is a true teacher.
Jack Haas, author of *The Way of Wonder*

1905047452 224pp **£10.99 $19.95**

Take Me To Truth
Undoing the Ego
Nouk Sanchez and Tomas Vieira

"Take Me To Truth" is not just a book - it's a revelation. Nouk Sanchez is a gifted spiritual teacher who knows what she is talking about and has a good idea of how to communicate her knowledge. The writing of Nouk and Tomas is uncompromising, exciting and strikingly consistent.
Gary R Renard, author of *The Disappearance of the Universe*

978-1-84694-0 256pp **£9.99 $19.95**

The Barefoot Indian
The Making of a Messiahress
Julia Heywood

The book is warm, funny, but altogether life changing. It teaches lessons that are infinitely valuable, on life itself and the nature of the cosmos and the ailments of the human race. They are so many answers, and my old self is itching to show off and tell you some, but I am not able to. The book is one you must journey through and reflect upon by yourself. A touching and life changing read, "The Barefoot Indian" is definitely one to pick up the next time you visit your local bookstore. It is an easy and essential read for all ages.
She Unlimited Magazine

1846940400 112pp **£7.99 $16.95**

The Bhagavad Gita
Alan Jacobs

Alan Jacobs has succeeded in revitalising the ancient text of the Bhagavad Gita into a form which reveals the full majesty of this magnificent Hindu scripture, as well as its practical message for today's seekers. His incisive philosophic commentary dusts off all the archaism of 1500 years and restores the text as a transforming instrument pointing the way to Self Realization.
Cygnus Review

1903816513 320pp **£12.99 $19.95**

The Book of One
Dennis Waite

A magisterial survey that belongs on the shelves of any serious student.
Scientific and Medical Network Review

1903816416 288pp **£9.99 $17.95**

The Essence of Reality
A Clear Awareness of How Life Works
Thomas Nehrer

Rarely has a human glimpsed beyond the confines of the self-aware mind to see the interactive flow of mind-value into Reality. Thomas Nehrer here goes beyond a glimpse to specify that flow, depicting Consciousness explicitly. The Essence of Reality illustrates that all of one's life – health, success, authority, abundance – reflect one's inner nature, leading the reader to see exactly how that works.

9781846940835 272pp **£11.99 $24.95**

The Good Remembering
A Message for our Times
Llyn Roberts

Llyn's work changed my life. "The Good Remembering" is the most important book I've ever read.
John Perkins, NY Times best selling author of *Confessions of an Economic Hit Man*

1846940389 196pp **£7.99 $16.95**

You Are the Light
John Martin Sahajananda

To the conventional theologian steeped in the Judaeo-Christian tradition, this book is challenging and may even be shocking at times. For mature Christians and thinkers from other faiths, it makes its contribution to an emerging Christian theology from the East that brings in a new perspective to Christian thought and vision.
Westminster Interfaith

1903816300 224pp **£9.99 $15.95**